Narcissism

How to Move On From Passive-Aggressive Covert Abuse - Includes Covert Narcissist and Narcissistic Abuse

Grace Horton

©Copyright 2021 – *Grace Horton* - All rights reserved

The content contained within this book may not be reproduced, duplicated, or transmitted without direct written permission from the author or the publisher.

Under no circumstances will any blame or legal responsibility be held against the publisher, or author, for any damages, reparation, or monetary loss due to the information contained within this book, either directly or indirectly.

Legal Notice

This book is copyright protected. This book is only for personal use. You cannot amend, distribute, sell, use, quote or paraphrase any part, or the content within this book, without the consent of the author-publisher.

Disclaimer Notice

Please note the information contained within this document is for educational and entertainment purposes only. All effort has been executed to present accurate, up to date, and reliable, complete information. No warranties of any kind are declared or implied. Readers acknowledge that the author is not engaging in the rendering of legal, financial, medical, or professional advice.

Table of Contents

Narcissistic Abuse 5

Introduction 6

Chapter 1 What is Narcissistic Abuse? 11

Chapter 2 How Narcissists Abuse 29

Chapter 3 Gaslighting 38

Chapter 4 Narcissist Target: Traits that Makes You a Prime Target for Narcissists 44

Chapter 5 Coping with a Narcissist 52

Chapter 6 Surviving Narcissistic Abuse 69

Chapter 7 Helping a Narcissist Recover 86

Chapter 8 The Narcissist and Empathy 94

Chapter 9 Healing from Narcissistic Abuse 109

Chapter 10 Dating After Leaving a Narcissist 119

Chapter 11 Case Study and its Implications 126

Conclusion 134

The Covert Narcissist 136

Introduction 137

Chapter 1: *Origins of a Narcissist* 139

Chapter 2: The Covert Narcissist 150

Chapter 3: *Am I a Narcissist?* 158

Chapter 4: *Falling in Love with a Narcissist* 164

Chapter 5: *Narcissistic Passive-Aggressiveness* 171

Chapter 6: *Living with a Narcissist? Do and Don'ts you Should Know About* 177

Chapter 7: *The Language of Narcissists* 183

Chapter 8: *Narcissist Abuse* 190

Chapter 9: *Gaslighting* 198

Chapter 10: *Stop the Narcissism* 205

Chapter 11: *A Hidden Narcissist Suffers Internally?* 212

Chapter 12: *The Narcissist's Target* 215

Chapter 13: *Narcissist and Relationships* 221

Chapter 14: *Empathy* 225

Chapter 15: *Co-dependency and Narcissists* 232

Chapter 16: *Dealing with a Narcissist* 239

Chapter 17: *Your Road to Recovery* 243

Chapter 18: *Long-Term Recovery* 250

Conclusion 257

Narcissistic Abuse

What the Victims Need to Know to Break the Cycle and Recovery from Emotional and Psychological Abuse

Bianca Sutton

Introduction

Narcissistic abuse is a form of abuse that is difficult to identify and heal from. Narcissists are natural born actors, and they use their special assets to manipulate their victims into believing their behavior is justified. They often come across as charismatic, likable, and charming in public, but there's another side to them that they only show behind closed doors where the true nature of their personality is revealed. According to the Merriam-Webster Dictionary, narcissistic abuse is: "The condition of suffering from chronic or repeated devaluation of self-worth by a primary caretaker, with the resulting in development of narcissistic personality traits."

While in essence this definition may be true, the root cause cannot be attributed to one person and narcissism can develop as a result of different factors that play a role in shaping personality. While some may argue that it is merely a manifestation of a personality disorder, others believe that upbringing and environment contribute to its development. It's not as simple as pointing a finger at one person and blaming him/her for the inevitable misery a victim or two may experience. At times, it's hard to detect, but if you see the signs of narcissism in any relationship, be it intimate or professional, let it be a warning that you might end up with someone who is abusive.

In current society, everyone easily comes across a narcissist. The internet has given us an easy way to seek out potential partners that we might not have otherwise found. Some people fall into bad relationships because they are not aware of the traits of a narcissist. This can be dangerous because a narcissistic can easily spot a potential victim and manipulate him/her by taking advantage of the fact that he/she might relate to them. The first sign that you might be in an abusive relationship is when your partner is always trying to get all the attention. When you don't pay any attention to him/her, they will use different strategies like creating drama or whatever it takes so you focus on them. A narcissist may be very jealous, controlling, and manipulative in an unhealthy manner.

A healthy relationship is one where both partners are well adjusted in a balanced manner. But when we start to recognize the signs of narcissistic behavior, it becomes easy to identify narcissistic traits. The signs to be aware of are:

1. Your partner is always trying to get your attention. This can be done through constant texting, calling you all the time, and even sending unwanted gifts that you don't need or want but are too polite or considerate to refuse.
2. Your partner has an over-inflated ego and characterizes himself/herself as a person who is intelligent and superior to most people in the world.

3. Your partner does not treat his/her victim with basic human respect and dignity. For example, if your partner insults you, he/she will never consider apologizing or making amends.
4. Your partner is condescending and superior in public but becomes very polite when alone with you.

In terms of relationships, narcissists thrive on control; they find it difficult to comprehend or accept that their victims have a definite opinion about certain issues. Therefore, it's normal that the victims be commanded to do certain things without being given any reason or explanation. They'll usually make abusive statements like, "When I shout you will do what I want," or "If you don't fall in line, nobody will love you." Narcissists tend to be possessive in relationships which can cause a lot of tension as they always think there's someone else whose attention is better than theirs.

One of the biggest issues people have with narcissism is that they feel as though they are being controlled by their partner rather than the other way round. While many might not see it as abuse, others would argue that while there is an element of control in most relationships, it shouldn't come across as abusive. While many people have the ability to be manipulative and controlling, it's the way that they go about it that is the biggest sign. This book will show you how not to get trapped in a relationship with a narcissist.

Narcissist is a word we come across almost every day, but what does it mean? In this book, we explored every point of it, and every angle was well researched to give you the best and well-compiled research on the subject. You may be struggling in your relationship, at home or with your friend and feel you are never enough. No matter how much you give it your best, you never really satisfy them, and you never reach the point they want you to. You feel like whatever you do is never good enough for them.

Well, this is the right book for you. You identify some characteristics of the typical narcissist, and now you will be able to understand the behaviors of some people and get to know why they do what they do. You may learn to accept the fact that you are not always the problem, but they are. Going deeper into this, you will know better how to handle such people. It might have been hard dealing with someone who demeans you all the time, is not able to understand you or even care what you are feeling.

You will know how to deal with a narcissist and live with them under the same roof without trying to please them. As wise man once said that at times, it is good to be a coward. When it comes a narcissist, you are actually not dealing with them at all, and you need to avoid these people at all costs. It's better to stick with others. We will give you some tips on how to prevent narcissist from entering your life or when you identify one, you know to run for your dear life before it is too late.

A narcissist can drain you and kill your self-esteem. to save yourself, stay away from them: that is the only way out. This will be a life-changing experience.

Chapter 1
What is Narcissistic Abuse?

Narcissists don't love themselves; they are driven by shame. It is an idealized picture they use to convince themselves that they embody what they admire. But deep down, a narcissistic feels a gap between the facade shown to the world and their ego-based shame. They work hard to prevent shame. This gap also applies to other offenders, but the narcissist uses defensive mechanisms that destroy normal conditions and cause pain and damage to the confidence of his loved ones. (To diagnose a narcissistic personality disorder, use "NPD").

Many narcissistic coping mechanisms are offensive; hence, the term "narcissistic abuse". However, someone can be abusive and not be a narcissist. Addicts and people with other mental disorders, such as bipolar disorder, antisocial personality disorder (sociopathy), and cross-border personality disorder are also abusive. Abuse is abuse, regardless of the diagnosis. If you're a victim of abuse, the biggest challenges are:

- Clear identification
- Building a support system
- Learn how to protect oneself

Abuse can be mental, physical, financial, spiritual or sexual. Here are some examples of abuse that you might not have detected:

Verbal violence: includes degradation, bullying, accusation, accusation, accusation, shame, demanding, orderly, threatening, criticizing, sarcasm, furious, averted, undermining, disrupting, blocking, and abusive. Note that many people sometimes use sarcasm, interrupt you, resist, criticize, blame or block. Consider the context, anger, and frequency of behavior before calling it narcissistic abuse.

Manipulation: generally affects someone who support self-centered and motivated goals. It often expresses a hidden aggression. Think of the "wolf in sheep's clothing". At first glance, the words appear harmless and they even complement each other; but underneath you feel humiliated or hostile. If your manipulation is entrenched, you may not recognize it as such.

Emotional extortion: include threats, anger, warnings, threats or punishment. It is a form of manipulation that casts doubt upon you. You feel a fear, duty and/or guilt, sometimes referred to as "FOG."

Gas Lighting: intentionally causes your suspicions to support your negative perception of reality or the belief that you are mentally incompetent.

Competition: competitive is high and insidious with a narcissist, sometimes with the use of unethical means. For example, cheating in a game.

Negative contrast: compare and contrasting you with narcissists or other people.

Sabotage: interfering with your efforts or relationships for revenge or personal gain.

Usage and objectification: using you for personal purposes regardless of your feelings or needs.

Recumbent: persistent scams without accountability or achieving the narcissist's goals.

Choice: things like money, sex, communication or love.

Ignoring : ignore the needs of a child for which the offender is responsible. Includes endangering children such as leaving a child in a potentially harmful situation.

Invasion of privacy: ignoring your personal borders by tracking you by phone or email; denying your physical privacy, chasing or follow you; ignoring the privacy you desire.

Character defamation: Spreading harmful gossip or lies about you to others.

Violence: blocking your movements, pulling you, throwing things, or destroying your property.

Financial abuse: includes controlling financial domination or emptying your finances by blackmailing, stealing, manipulating or gambling, or even creating debt in your name or selling your personal property.

Isolation: isolate you from friends, family, or access to external services and support through control, manipulation, verbal abuse, assassination, or other forms of abuse.

Malignant Narcissism and Sociopathy

A person with excessive narcissistic qualities who behaves harmfully and hostilely is considered to have "harmful narcissism". Harmful narcissists do not suffer guilt. They can be sadistic and enjoy causing pain. They can be so competitive and unprincipled that they exhibit anti-social behavior. Paranoia places them in a defensive attack mode as a means of self-defense.

Malignant narcissism is akin to sociopathy. Sociopaths have been crushed or damaged in some way so they exhibit narcissistic traits; but not all narcissists are sociopathic. Their motivations are different. While narcissists are ideal persons to be admired, sociopaths reach only for their self-sufficient agenda. They have to win at all costs and do not think about violating social norms and laws. They don't care about people like narcissists do.

Narcissists do not want to be abandoned. They depend on the approval of others, but sociopaths easily release relationships that do not serve them. Although some narcissists think about achieving their goals, they are usually more reactive than sociopaths who figure out their cold and evil plans.

You may have asked yourself at least a thousand times, "Why am I staying in this madness?" You may have come up with a possible answer - the fear of being alone - while acknowledging that your experience is not necessarily real fear itself. By assessing why you have remained in such an emotionally destructive relationship, you might conclude that although you prefer company; you also realize that discomfort and emotional pain come with the narcissist in your life.

You realize that you would be lonely by giving up this reality, and you distance yourself from grief to survive. You can experience, at least temporarily, some relief from emotional pain and discomfort. Yet it is unlike the emotional pain experienced by the narcissist who as an emotional addict and despite your efforts to attract their attention through various activities gets no relief.

You've found that you can be in the midst of your beloved family and friends, attend a long-awaited concert at a professional sporting event, go to a beautiful beach with perfect weather, yet have a broken heart. Unfortunately, you are unique in this experience. People advise, "Life continues. Come on. Stop apologizing. Don't give this person time to think about them. They certainly don't think about you." If all the well-meaning outsiders just knew how hard you have tried! Why are you going into this world of fear? Have you been told, "You must love pain because you are the one who chooses to stay with a narcissistic emotional addict?" It doesn't make sense to others, nor does it make sense to you.

You keep asking why? That's a good thing because only you can find the answer. Your journey is so unique. Will this curse ever be a blessing? If you survive, yes it will. The struggle, if you're still involved with a narcissistic emotional addict, is whether you want to survive. This does not mean that you are going to die, but it is also a possibility. What is being said here is that you existed before crossing paths with a narcissistic emotional abuser. You used to laugh, create, jump and run, smile and enjoy simple things in life. After joining a narcissistic r emotions, the colors, sounds, and smells of life have been lost to you. You live and breathe but feel dead inside, except for the pain stomach pain. Nothing makes more sense. You ask again, Why do I stay in this chaos? Why do I love them so much? Why do I love them more than my own life? Why? There is the possible joy of the "golden egg". Maybe they promises you to travel, own a house or build a bigger, nicer house. Do they have a lot of money? Does it make you feel like no friend has given you any similar feeling? When you are in their presence, no one else matters.

Think about it. What do they have on you? It's like a curse with an invisible power. You feel the curse attracting the narcissistic emotional abuser. It is like being in a prison cell with the door open, but you can't walk and stay outside. What kind of golden egg do they have? What did they do to make you start to believe that you can't live without them? They may deny this reality, even if you have clear evidence to support your case. Do you think somewhere in your mind that you are the winner of a revered golden goose if they choose you instead of all others?

Finding and understanding the golden egg with the narcissistic emotional culprit can be a challenge. Discovering your golden egg will reveal your most important uncertainties. This fear is so great in you that you risk death. You choose to endure abuse instead of dealing with it and making it become too real. It is said that most people die with the music that is still there. Do you have the courage to be yourself?

If you seek and find the golden egg with a narcissistic emotional abuser in your life, your curse will become a blessing. Be encouraged and dare to be you.

TYPES OF NARCISSISTS

Full-Blown Narcissist

A full-blown narcissist is the type that is not predictable nor preventable. These are types of people who strike when it is least expected, and nothing can be done to stop them. This is mainly characterized by an arrogance that disrupts and blows things out of proportion. Full-blown narcissism is the last stage where all the characteristics of narcissism have been blended and the victim, most of the time, turns out to be violent and uncontrollable. They can throw things everywhere or even mess because of a pure provocation at anything you do; a full-blown narcissist will always find a reason to get mad.

Covert Narcissist

A covert narcissist is the inverse of the overt narcissist in that they crave and demand self-importance and admiration, unlike the overt type who always needs to be right. Covert narcissistic behaviors are soft and subtle. Although they crave fame and recognition, they do it in ways that do not infringe another person's rights. The only difference between a covert and a full-blown narcissist is that the former chooses not to outwardly manifest their longing while the latter are fully intent on letting their demands known. In other words, coverts are an introverted version of full-blown narcissists although both fantasize about their self-worthiness and self-importance; the only difference is the way they manifest them. Many people have fallen victim of a covert narcissist because of the insidious way they work; you will never understand the harm they bring on their victims until much of it has been witnessed.

The primary characteristic of the overt narcissist is passive self-importance. They don't inflate their quest and thirst for admiration and importance, and they get them anyhow. Another trait of the covert narcissist is shaming others. Coverts never want to carry the blame, and they would rather shame and blame others for elevating themselves to be seen as of a higher caliber.

People With Narcissistic Tendencies

There are people who are narcissists, and there are people who are not narcissists but have narcissistic tendencies. One can manifest the traits of narcissists without being one. For instance, they can be self-centered with low empathy, and still they are not narcissists. So what qualifies one to be a narcissist, and what differentiates people with narcissistic traits from true narcissists?

People with narcissistic tendencies divide the populace into two: those to be looked up to and those to be looked down on. Unlike narcissists, people with narcissistic tendencies are realistic but instead have qualities worth emulating and others that are worth nothing.

The primary traits of people with narcissistic tendencies are domineering and always appear to know it all, but they will not be battling with self-esteem issues that the narcissists are fighting and grappling with. The only difference between the narcissists and people with narcissistic tendencies is that the people with tendencies have the capacity to see people as a mixture of good and evil and be able to associate themselves with the good ones while having nothing to do with the bad ones.

Narcissistic abuse is not exclusive. This kind of physical torment has happened to millions of people in the world. If it has happened to you too or is already happening to you now, know that you are not alone. You may be asking yourself, "Why me?" You might be feeling that this woeful experience is only happening to you. You might even blame yourself and feel like you are not good enough. But the truth is, you are not alone, and it is not your fault.

If you can, research about the experience you have been going through. Check on the internet about it. Take the next step and reach out for help. Talk to trusted people like professional counselors, experienced therapists, psychologists, friends, and family members that you can trust. You can even contact trauma facilities. Your healing will start immediately. You begin to see the reality of what has been happening to you. Seek help soon, especially if you are experiencing extreme symptoms like suicidal thoughts.

Make safety plans if you begin to see signs of people close to you becoming violent. In an abusive relationship, a trauma bond develops between the abuser and the abused. This is due to the hopelessness instilled in the abused person. However, sometimes moving and finding safety is less expensive than staying and taking in more abuse. It is possible to reach a point of recovery, with no or limited contact with the victim. The road to recovery is not easy, but it is worth it. The final destination will be attaining your freedom and getting yourself back on your feet.

In a nutshell, this is how narcissist abuse looks like: your happiness is denied, you lose your self-identity and have no freedom of expression. You are only there to listen and not to talk. You are to be seen not to heard. Your reality is warped and distorted. You are abused, threatened, manipulated, lied to, ridiculed, and taken through some ugly experiences. Then you are made to believe that you imagine things. You are called "mad" and told that you only have yourself to blame.

Perhaps you were even replaced and thrown out. Then you were lured back into the same cycle of abuse, this time with more painful experiences. You are stalked, harassed, and made to stay with the abuser by force. The most painful part is that the person doing all this to you is the very person who is supposed to protect you from it. It is the person you trusted and had hope in.

These are not the ups and downs of a healthy relationship no matter how much you might want to convince yourself that your companion is unique. This is an abusive companion who will break your soul, kill your sense of self, or even worse, your physical being. Other people will not understand, for you may not have physical scars to show. All you have are the internal wounds, fractured memories, and mental battles. This sounds very horrific. But don't be scared as it is possible to get yourself together. You can get your life back.

GETTING YOURSELF TOGETHER

Here are tips that will help you get yourself together.

Game Changing

Narcissists sabotage their victim's minds. They will make you believe that all that should matter to you is doing what they want without a second thought. Forget yourself and start singing songs of adoration to them. Sadly, no matter how much you give yourself to them, they are never satisfied. They get you on your toes at every moment. You keep thinking which of the next demands you should meet. Eventually, you bend to their desires. Don't get too involved in the narcissist monopoly conversations about what you have done wrong. Give yourself a break. tell yourself that it is not true. Detach fast and don't swallow that verbal poison.

Misrepresenting Your Thoughts and Words

Toxic narcissists perceive themselves as mind readers. They think they know what other people are thinking. They say things like, "I know you, I know what you want to say, I know how you think." They will put words into your mouth. They complete your sentences even before they begin. Also, before you get a chance to call out their misbehavior, they already are ready with excuses. You can only think about what they want you to believe, and you can only say what they want you to say. This is not good of course. The narcissist never evaluates what is really happening because they can't and won't come into terms with reality. They react to their triggers, created in their world of delusions.

State your case firmly and walk away with no more arguments. Do not give them a chance to shift the blame to you. The more you entrain them, the more they convince you that you should be ashamed of accusing them, and this could give them more rights to future abuse.

Changing the Subject

This is their common tactic. A narcissist will never want to be held accountable for any misdeed. They always redirect the conversation. The redirection often lands on one of the mistakes of the accuser. Narcissists are never afraid of pulling out your past mistakes, even if it committed ten years ago. They make it look so bad and render their accusers powerless by holding them accountable for everything. When this diversion happens, redirect it back to the original topic. State firmly that is not what you wanted to discuss. If they still insist on blaming you, stop the conversation and keep yourself busy with something else.

Smearing

A narcissist is capable of abusing deliberately so that you will react, and then they will use your reactions against you. They slander you and report back to anybody who cares to listen. They create stories to show that you are the abuser and they are the victim. Ironically, they accuse you of doing the wrong things they themselves do as a cover-up not to get the blame.

When this happens, seek help and avoid confrontation with the abuser. They will provoke and hurt you until you can't take it anymore. Then, they watch and wait for your reactions, which they will use against you. In case you seek justice, it is good to talk to a lawyer familiar with Narcissist Personality Disorder.

Triangulating

The narcissist may bring the views and opinions of other people into the dynamics of the relationship to validate their harmful actions and invalidate the reactions of their significant other. They triangulate them to parents, siblings, coworkers, strangers, and everyone else that matters. Triangulation can include love triangles. This influence other partners to use their opinions against you. This leaves you hanging, feeling insecure, and full of self-doubt. This is a tactic to disorient you from the toxic narcissist's behavior. It leads you to believe in their self-perception that they are desirable and perfect people. The narcissist also likes to report false information of what others say about you. This leaves you questioning yourself and feeling terrible about who you are.

To overcome triangulation, try your best to seek your validation. You can also reverse-triangulate a narcissist by gaining support from another person who is not influenced by the narcissist. The third party the narcissist is triangulating with is also triangulating with you. You are being played all around.

Preemptive Defense

A toxic narcissist likes to give themselves endless praise that has no basis. Despite having very dysfunctional behaviors, they want to show themselves up as a nice guy. Their conversations are full of boastful statements about how good they are and how other people should be associated with them. They overestimate their ability to be compassionate and kind.

These abusers expect everyone to see them as they see themselves. They cannot stand anybody who sees them as anything less than the right person. That is why their affinity for praise and affirmation never ends. They tell people to trust them even when they have not built a foundation for trust. Their false mask slips off as the abuse gets full brown and the cold and contemptuous personality is revealed. The victim becomes frustrated.

Your preemptive defense can be countered, so focus not on what the narcissist says, but what they do. Investigate why they insist on being a good person. You will find it is because they know you should not trust them, and they are afraid you will get to know this.

Sugarcoating

Malicious people find it fun to mess with others. They test and tease other people's mind then make it a joke. As discussed, narcissists are capable of squeezing your insecurities out of you, then document and use it in the future. They tell you something harmful to measure your reaction. They say they did not mean it and pretend to be innocent. This leaves you confused and vulnerable to future attacks. At this stage, you are being baited to stop being defensive altogether.

Your instincts can tell you when there are baiting and sugar coating. When they say something wrong and then ask you to take it lightly, that is a red flag. Do not listen to false flattery. Internalize what you feel about it and leave some space for detaching.

Being under the narcissist's manipulation is no joke. It is better to know how to counter them as early as possible. If you are already in it, take the first step. Be bold and seek all the help you can. If legal advice is required, do not hesitate to get it.

Chapter 2
How Narcissists Abuse

Many people are unaware of the abuse they suffer from a narcissist or just don't know that what they're going through is abuse because narcissistic abuse can be difficult to identify. Narcissistic behavior goes beyond being simply selfish and egocentric; it crosses into manipulation and brainwashing where the victim loses all sense of self-worth and independence.

Narcissists often spend time charming their victims while simultaneously criticizing them in private. They get you to invest your energy, emotions, and money in them then discard you without remorse when the relationship ends. It's a form of mental and emotional abuse that can leave the victim feeling confused, exhausted, and stressed. They may develop into Post-Traumatic Stress Disorder (PTSD) where depression, flashbacks and anxiety are not uncommon.

When someone is victimized by a narcissist for any length of time, it creates long-term effects on that person's life. The victim will have to suffer from the aftermath of narcissistic abuse for years after the relationship is over. They might spend years trying to make sense of what happened in their relationship with the narcissist, trying to understand how someone they loved so much could treat them so horrendously. They might have to bury their feelings deep inside so as not upset other people around them. They might have low self-esteem, feel worthless or guilty, and blame themselves for the narcissist's abusive behavior.

It's normal for someone who suffered from narcissistic abuse to be confused and conflicted because they often idealized their abuser in the beginning of the relationship. They are reluctant to admit that the person they idolized is actually a dangerous abuser who has now completely shattered their self-esteem. Many victims think that they will be blamed by others when they start talking about how they were abused by a narcissist, so they keep quiet.

The following are ways in which narcissists abuse people:

Extreme Jealousy

The narcissist has an inverse sense of sexuality where they constantly feel inferior and jealous because they need constant admiration and attention to feed their fragile ego. They will often exhibit extreme paranoia about their partner's feelings for others, even if they have absolutely no reason to doubt them. If you are in a relationship with a narcissist, or had one in the past, then you probably remember countless late night fights because they got jealous over someone just trying to be friendly.

Using Guilt and Emotional Blackmail

The narcissist will use guilt, threats, and emotional blackmail to get what they want. The narcissist will accuse you of doing things that you probably didn't do (even though you wouldn't have done it if they hadn't asked). Narcissists know how to manipulate people by using fear and threats. They will also use guilt. You might have done something wrong in the narcissist's eyes, but they won't say anything directly; instead, they just accuse you of being a bad person and trying to escape them.

When you're in a relationship with a narcissist, you will often feel guilty like you're in the wrong. You might be feeling guilty about something they accused you of doing that you didn't do, or it could just be the way they accuse you of what is happening that makes you feel bad.

You might feel as though it was your fault for some reason, but the narcissist is the one who acted like a sociopathic child and has completely destroyed their partner's self-esteem. they continue to do so by assailing their partner with narcissistic rage. It's only normal to feel stressed when going through narcissistic abuse because it involves multiple forms of abuse all at once.

You may feel like everything you do is wrong, that you're a horrible person, and no one else would want to be with you. These are all normal feelings after being abused by a narcissist. The narcissist will do anything they can to make you feel guilty because it makes it easier for them to control you and keep you in the relationship.

Degradation and Humiliation

When you're in a relationship with a narcissist, you will feel small and worthless. You might even feel like you don't exist or your needs are unimportant. The narcissist will do anything to make sure that they feel superior to you in every way. They may constantly put you down or humiliate you in private by making jokes at your expense or by making fun of the things important to you.

Abusive Comments and Verbal Abuse

The narcissist won't say anything directly when they want to get their point across. It's all indirect, subtle, and oftentimes disguised as a joke or by making fun of you. If you start saying something, the narcissist might laugh at you because they know that will make you feel bad, and it makes it easier for them to control you.

The narcissist will find a way to make your life difficult without directly admitting it. They will use passive aggressive comments when they want to say something directly to piss you off without giving anything up in return. They have learned to never say anything in plain sight unless they want other people to know that they are being abusive towards their partner.

This also creates fear in the victim. They often cannot tell if they are being abused because they are so afraid of the consequences of it not working out. This is more common in people who haven't been abused before. Many times this abuse will come in the form of passive aggressive remarks or emotional abuse which can be harder to spot and prove.

Projection and Accusations

The narcissist will accuse you of things without actually saying anything directly to you. Of course, they will usually accuse you of doing things you probably didn't do, but it is equally likely they did do so as a way for them to exert control over your life.

Projective Identification and Provoking Defensiveness

The narcissist may start to make comments that are strange without really saying anything. They may accuse you of being a certain way or having certain traits that they actually have themselves. This is very common with abusive narcissistic relationships because the narcissist often has an extreme form of insecurity and feels that they need to prove their worth by destroying the other person instead of building a stronger relationship as a reciprocal exchange.

Engulfing, Entitlement, and Abusive Dependency

In this relationship dynamic, the narcissist will become so entwined in your life that it becomes difficult to live your own life. They will check up on you constantly and become the center of your life. They will oftentimes not leave you alone unless they think you are cheating on them or something else is wrong in your life.

They rarely give you your space. The narcissist wants to control what you do, who you are with, and what kind of friends you have. Even if it's not really that bad in their minds, they will often try to manipulate situations or people so it feels like everything is falling apart around them without actually doing anything bad themselves to make it happen.

Unreasonable Expectations of Reciprocity and Unpredictability

The narcissist is extremely unpredictable. They are very likely to do or say something that doesn't make any sense. They may give you gifts and be extremely kind and then turn around and talk about how much they hate you. This is because they feel entitled to have something when they want it, regardless of the fact that other people in their environment also exist on the same planet.

They will give you their attention when it suits them and then ignore you for days. They will demand a lot from their partners but not really give much in return. They will expect you to be on call for them 24/7 and have no problem making you feel like your life revolves around them.

Excessive Need for Admiration

Narcissists demand a lot of admiration and attention. They have a big "I'm the center of attention" mindset that can make it very difficult for their partners to get any attention or love from the other people in their lives. This means that they will likely become jealous if you friends, and they are not included in these relationships. They will get angry and upset if you take time doing things that don't involve them. That's a deal breaker for me.

And finally, the one thing that gets to me is when they talk bad about others behind their backs. Then I get really mad and upset. This is like cutting off your nose to spite your face. It's so stupid and shows a lack of respect. It is totally selfish and inconsiderate. Don't do it!

If you are married or in a committed relationship, only talk to your partner and other people in confidence or with full disclosure…it kills a friendship real fast when the person you are talking about finds out that you were talking behind their back.

When someone is narcissistic, it's easy to get sucked in. It seem like they are the only person you can count on. They will be very charming and personable with you in the beginning of the relationship because they want to seem like a person who values your friendship and interest.

This is usually when you become the victim of their manipulation and abuse. It might even take years for the full extent of it to hit home. It is very likely that you'll wake up one day and realize that you were deceived. You might be afraid to confront them because they are usually very good at making you feel guilty and that it's your fault you were abused.

The narcissist will use your emotions and heart against you. They will say things that make it seem like they care about you when they are actually just trying to get more control over your life to get what they want. If you are dating a narcissist, you need to walk away before they destroy your life. They will eat their way through your self-esteem and make sure that you never trust another person again.

Narcissistic abuse is extremely dangerous, and it is wise to walk away from the relationship. The forces of narcissism are scary, and if you let them get a hold of you, they will destroy your life. Your self-esteem won't be the only thing they will take. Chances are, they'll also destroy your sanity and self-worth. Please don't make the same mistakes I did and don't let a narcissist continue to abuse you.

Chapter 3
Gaslighting

Narcissists are absolute masters of manipulation. They can turn your whole life upside down in the blink of an eye. Unfortunately, what people don't often realize is that this abuse doesn't end there; it can continue for years after the relationship is over. This chapter will examine a common form of abuse from narcissists called gaslighting, which causes victims to second guess themselves and their perceptions.

Gaslighting is a form of emotional abuse where manipulators get in your head and convince you that what you know and see with your own eyes isn't real; it's all just happening in your head. This type of abuse is so effective because it happens gradually over time, making it very hard to notice that you're being manipulated.

What Does Gaslighting Look Like?

Gaslighting abuse manipulates memories, thoughts and emotions. It happens when someone says something that isn't true as if it is, but you are so confused that you begin second-guessing yourself. One common tactic the narcissist uses to gaslight his victims is called "blanking" the victim. This means that at certain points, the narcissist will try to erase a person from their memory or pretend like they never existed; this includes pretending like certain events or conversations never happened. This type of gaslighting can be especially damaging because the narcissist is essentially denying his partner's reality.

Gaslighting also includes twisting a victim's perception of their own reality. One obvious form is lying to someone, but it can be much more subtle than that. Let's say both David and Brandi are at home in their apartment when Jane, who they know, comes to the door to drop something off as she often does.

In this situation, Brandi has answered the door and is startled to see Jane there; she thought she was alone with David who is reading. Now Jane walks in and sees David reading a book instead of being on his computer as he usually is at this time of the day. Jane questions David and asks him what he is doing. David says he was doing some research for work, which is true. However, Brandi heard this and thought to herself, Really? He's telling Jane that he was doing research for work when he said only thirty minutes ago he said that he was going to take a break from the computer to read? This is where things get tricky. Brandi continues to have doubts about David's claims even though they were all true.

The most extreme form of gaslighting can potentially cause the victim to start questioning their own sanity, making them think that they themselves are crazy. Gaslighting is one of the most toxic forms of emotional abuse because it so completely infects your reality. It takes a lot of strength to stand up to this type of manipulation because you have to convince yourself that what you know and see with your own two eyes really happened. If you begin to doubt yourself, it makes it easier for the manipulator to get away with his or her abuse.

How Does Gaslighting Happen?

Gaslighting abuse isn't just a one-time occurrence; it happens over an extended period of time and gives the abuser the chance to manipulate his or her victim over and over again. It starts by slowly gaining trust to access the partner's life. Once she has gained access, she begins to slowly confuse and manipulate the victim over time. The gaslighting abuser changes their stories, contradicts themselves, and twists reality to make it sound like the victim is delusional.

The abuser also starts other arguments to deflect attention away from their own lies. At this point, the victim begins to have doubts about themselves and what they believe is real, which causes them to question their own reality. The manipulator then uses these doubts against the victim while continuing the abuse.

How to Deal with Gaslighting

There are three main ways to deal with gaslighting. The first is not to be controlled by it because when you are gaslighted, you are essentially being controlled by the abuser. You are not in control of yourself, making it extremely difficult to escape the situation. The second way is to learn how to recognize the signs and tell people what's going on. This will make it easier for your friends and family members see what is happening. The third way is to have a support system in place while confronting your abuser; it's hard enough to deal with an abusive relationship without support from those around you.

How to Deal with Your Own Doubts

In every abusive situation, the victim becomes the person they're trying to escape. They lose their identity, and they don't know themselves anymore. This is why it's so important to take time for yourself to get back in touch with who you really are. Don't let someone else define you - it's your life. Take some time for yourself and reflect on what you want and need out of life; this will help you rediscover parts of yourself that may have gotten lost in the abuse. If any part of your identity has been tainted by gaslighting, it's time to put it behind you.

Recovery

If you're the victim of gaslighting abuse, don't give up. It's so important to remember that there is no such thing as a perfect relationship; if you have one, then it's not yours. Your partner should support and help you grow into your best self and not manipulate you into believing what they think is real.

If your relationship feels like it's impossible to break out of, then reach out for help. You do not have to face it alone; there are many resources that can help you along your journey to freedom. You are worth the fight, and no one has the right to deny your reality but you.

Gaslighting can happen to anyone regardless of gender, age or position. However, it is a well-known fact that women are more prone to this type of abuse than men, and the three most common types of gaslighters are parents, siblings and partners. Older women (50–85 years) experience the highest rates of physical and sexual violence from younger male partners in intimate relationships when they are also experiencing ageism.

Gaslighting may be described as an extreme case of emotional abuse by manipulation. The abuser wants the victim to question their own feelings, instincts, and sanity by distorting the truth. Gaslighting abuse is often subtle. Its victims are led to question their own reactions through "family" or "friend" manipulation, usually portrayed as a joke, which can lead to anxiety, depression, and ultimately substance abuse problems. These can be the more severe manifestations of the abuse.

The victims of gaslighting don't recognize it as an act of violence until they have been deceived for so long that their former reality is distorted, and they think the new reality truly exists. This is often the reason why a victim doesn't come forward because they feel certain that no one would believe them.

The abuser also manages to make the victim's situation seem more critical than it actually is, which causes emotional distress. It is no wonder that the victim is more prone to using substances to cope with their situation or escape. Many abusers have even been known to exploit their victim's substance abuse problems for financial gain.

Chapter 4
Narcissist Target: Traits that Makes You a Prime Target for Narcissists

First, it is important to note that the popular notion that narcissists target weak, desperate women or men is nothing short of misleading. Also, being a victim of narcissistic abuse is never the victim's fault by any means. Narcissists are emotional predators and the fact that you're a human makes you automatically vulnerable to their antics. That said, it makes sense to identify the traits that narcissists identify in their targets so that potential victims can better protect themselves and sever ties early on, especially when they realize they are being targeted for exploitation.

When you consider these traits, you'll realize how wonderful they are, especially if allowed to blossom in a healthy and loving relationship. Sadly, a narcissist will only use them to manipulate, exploit ,and damage their victims. Below are some of the traits that narcissists look out for in potential victims:

1. Conscientiousness
2. Empathy
3. Integrity
4. Resilience

5. A high degree of sentimentality

6. Conscientiousness

Many people do not realize this, but one of the prime qualities a narcissist looks for is the ability of the potential victim to be conscientious. Truth be told, conscientious people are always concerned about the wellbeing of others, and they always carry out their obligation. The reason they are vulnerable to narcissists is that their decisions are tied to their conscience and, sadly, they project their sense of morality onto the narcissist, assuming that he will do the same.

Narcissists are very manipulative; they know how easy it is to exploit people who are conscientious enough to worry about other people's needs. They know that a conscientious person is one of the very few people that would grant them numerous chances, give them benefit of doubt, and even care more about them than their personal needs.

Narcissists love to target conscientious people for romantic relationships because they are aware of the fact that conscientious people see caretaking as an obligation, especially in relationships. They know that these people are ready to fulfill their obligations even if they feel endangered or if it puts them in harm's way.
Dr. George Simon, in his book, Personalities Prone to Narcissistic Manipulation, said that disturbed individuals most often target

those who possess two qualities that they, themselves, don't possess. These traits are excessive agreeableness being very conscientious. People with these traits tend to defer to others, such as the narcissist, by complying with their demands and manipulation. Ironically, those who possess a conscience are more vulnerable to those who do not. Shame and guilt are the primary tools or weapons used by those who manipulate others, but in order for that to work, you have to have the capacity for these traits in the first place.

Empathy

The joy of every narcissist is to encounter an empathic victim because narcissists, in general, do not get a constant narcissistic supply of attention, praise, resources, etc. from people who lack empathy - like themselves. Thus, the importance of securing a narcissistic target cannot be overemphasized.

Narcissists cannot show empathy towards others, but they carefully target people who have a great deal. The physical and emotional validation that empathic people give narcissists help maintain their bloated egos and feelings of authority, or else they practically starve and renew their hunt for a new source of supply.

When you put everything into consideration, you'll realize that empathic people are the opposite of narcissists, and their attitude helps to empower narcissists in their abuse cycle. For example, the fact that an empath is always willing to see the narcissist's perspective even at the height of abuse is something that maintains the abuse cycle over and over. As if that is not enough, narcissists identify with empathic people because they know that they're the ideal audience for their pity ploys even after highly abusive incidents.

If you happen to be an empathic person, understand that narcissists believe they can just put out a faux apology or sob story to write off their abuse. They know you'll always see reasons for their toxic behaviors and even make excuses on their behalf. They depend on your God-given ability to forgive and sympathize with them irrespective of the ill treatments they've subjected you to in the past.

Most times, narcissists escape retribution and accountability for their actions because they appeal to the empathy of their victims. It is very hard to pretend to be who you are not, and as such, empathic people, being who they are, always second-guess their decisions to punish the narcissists for their actions because they feel an unbearable amount of guilt when they see the narcissist prosecuted (either by society or law). Thus, they are always inclined to protect their abusers as opposed to exposing them to the world as to who they truly are.

Integrity

This might sound very funny, but narcissists are incredibly attracted to people who keep to their word. When they come in contact with people of integrity, they see a lot of attributes they can exploit for their own gain. For example, if it is not in the moral code of a victim to cheat or give up on a relationship prematurely, who stands to benefit? The narcissist, who is morally and mentally impoverished!

While the victims feel morally apprehensive about betraying the relationship, executing retaliation, or even withdrawing from their supposed obligations to the narcissists, the narcissist in question maintains zero remorse for harming their victims. The victim possesses a rare gift that can be of benefit to them and their partners in a healthy and productive relationship. However, this same gift becomes a weapon in the hands of a narcissist – a deadly weapon used to destroy their self-worth and self-belief.

Resilience

The most painful part about being a victim of narcissistic abuse is the realization that you weren't even wrong most times. As a victim of narcissistic abuse, your ability to bounce back from your abuser's acts is something that strengthens your bond with him.

Resilient people, e.g. childhood abuse survivors, are highly effective sources for the narcissist because they have a very high threshold for pain and abuse.

Resilience is a very good quality to possess, especially when faced with adversities of life, but in an abusive relationship, the victim's resilience is exploited and used against him/her to keep them enslaved in the abuser's web of deceit and manipulation.

Even though resilient people are more aware of the dangers of their environments, they still find it difficult to give up on their abusers even after multiple incidents. Typically, they will choose to disregard their instincts and fight for their relationship by assuming the role of a "fighter" or "savior," as they put in energy to keep an unsustainable relationship afloat.

The saddest part about the resilient victim is that there are times when they even quantify their love by the amount of abuse they've suffered at the hands of their abusers. Unknown to them, this occurs because they have successfully developed an abuse bond with the toxic and abusive partner.

High degree of sentimentality

There is no gainsaying that narcissists are overbearing, petty, and manipulative. Thus, targets who are sentimental and capable of falling deeply in love, are extremely appealing to narcissists because they know they can use love-bombing (the use of extreme praise and flattery to groom a victim) to easily manipulate them.

During the early stages of narcissistic relationships, narcissists shower their victims with so much love and attention: the idea is to secure their trust and appeal to their craving for love. It is a strategy that works very well for them! They intentionally create sweet memories that they want their victims to romanticize during future periods of abuse.

Narcissists love to play with their victim's emotions; they know they can get their victims hooked before they start to withdraw by creating a fraudulent "soulmate" effect that will cripple their victims and leave them wanting things to be as they were during the early stages of the relationship.

Narcissists find it very easy to trick empathic and sentimental people – the only thing they do is fraud their victims into believing they're kicking off a meaningful, long-term relationship. It is very normal for people to want to maintain long term, healthy relationships, but it becomes a problem when a predatory narcissist is involved.

Why did the narcissist target you? You have something the narcissist wants (lifestyle, power, money, position). In a narcissistic relationship, certain things come into play. First of all, it begins with a hook – a dream – and most times you think it is all about you and your wellbeing, but the truth is that the narcissist is all about control.

There are occasions when the narcissist will appear to be helpful, but when things don't go as planned, the tables turn on you. However, when you realize the pattern and opt to hold the narcissist accountable for his actions, things get out of hands and degenerate rapidly.

Chapter 5
Coping with a Narcissist

Being able to identify a narcissist is just the beginning. Once you recognize that you have one in your life, the next step is knowing how to overcome the experience and its associated consequences. It can be emotionally and mentally challenging to be around a person with narcissism. It is imperative not to delay dealing with the situation properly to minimize potential negative effects.

Dealing with a Narcissist

Dealing with a narcissist is something that truly takes practice. It takes a different tack than those without narcissism, and since this is not an issue you deal with frequently with multiple people, there is a learning curve. Never discount yourself. This is what they want, but there are ways to ensure that you are creating and maintaining the right boundaries.

Do Not Give in to Their Fantasy

A narcissist builds a fantasy life, and when dealing with them, it is important not to fall into the fantasy. They can be charming so it can be hard to resist them. It does not take long to essentially get lost in their web. At first, you might feel important and special, but this never lasts. Keep the following in mind:

- They will not fulfill your needs. In fact, what you need and want will not even be recognized. A narcissist views your value as what you can do to satiate their ego.

- Pay attention to how they treat others. You will see that they are not afraid to manipulate, lie, disrespect and hurt other people. Eventually, this behavior and treatment will trickle down to you.

- While it is not easy, the rose-colored glasses have to come off to evaluate how they are truly treating you. When you care about someone, denial is the easiest route to take concerning their true character, but this has to be put aside.

- Don't forget about your dreams. When you are close to a narcissist, it is easy to get swept up in their delusions and fantasy. Do not lose yourself or you may find it hard to regain control.

Set Boundaries and Stick to Them

One of the biggest elements of a healthy relationship is setting healthy boundaries and sticking to them. Of course, a narcissist does not understand boundaries, so this can be tricky. Remember that your relationships with others should be built on a foundation of mutual respect and care. While you will not get what you give, you still have to approach the relationship like any other. This will reduce the chances of your boundaries being violated.

For example, a narcissist is not shy about taking what they want. You might have a female friend who is a narcissist who just raids your closet and takes anything at any time. In a normal friendship, this friend would ask first, but narcissists do not ask permission. They feel they deserve anything they want, and this includes anything you have.

If you have had a relationship with a narcissist for a while, you surely can see their pattern of not respecting boundaries. To change this, make a plan based on what you hope to achieve. Then, consider how you will enforce the plan and what the consequences will be should the narcissist violate your boundaries. The most important thing is that you stand firm and do not give into the needs of the narcissist. Let them know when your boundaries have been crossed.

Be prepared for relationship changes. A narcissist is not a big fan of people who don't admire them and give into their every whim. They want to call all the shots, and they want you to prop them up. Once you start creating boundaries, how they treat you is likely to change because they will not be happy about you standing up for yourself.

They may try to punish you, demean you, or go in the opposite direction and use fake charm to manipulate you into going back to giving them what they want. To maintain the friendship, you might take a gentle approach to boundary setting. For example, instead of just abruptly changing things and being harsh when explaining why, plan what to say and then deliver the message in a way that is clear, calm, gentle and respectful. If the conversation is not going as planned, simply walk away. Do not continue to engage or allow the person to try and manipulate you into going back to your old habits of giving in.

Avoid Taking Things Personally

This will be one of the hardest things you do, but it is important. A narcissist is not purposely trying to hurt you. This is just who they are, and they are unable to see fault in their behavior. Remember that their actions, behaviors, and emotions are not about you. It is all about them.

A narcissist will try and create a version of you that is easiest for them to control. Work on your self-esteem and know your worth so their view of you does not become how you see yourself. Let them keep their own negativity and do not allow it to change how you feel about yourself.

This also means that you need to know who you are. A narcissist is not able to admit that they have weaknesses, and they overinflate their strengths. However, you need to take an honest look at yourself. If a narcissist is attacking one of your strengths, you can simply walk away. You know it is something you are good at. Be proud of it and do not allow them to make you feel inferior.

Do not argue with them. This will be hard when the natural instinct is to defend yourself when someone is attacking you. Remember that a narcissist is not rational and no amount of logic will change this. Simply state calmly that you disagree and then walk away.

Lastly, never look to a narcissist for approval. Even if they tell you nice things, they are only doing it to manipulate and gain control over you. As long as you know your worth and have good self-esteem, you do not need them to approve of anything you do or think.

Find a Good Support System
A narcissist is never going to be a good support person for you. However, you do need support when dealing with someone like this in your life. If they are close to you and have been in your life

a while, the first step is learning what a healthy relationship is. It is about mutual respect and give and take. With a narcissist, you only give, and they only take.

Focus your time on those who give you love, respect, and honesty. This will help you to see who you truly are so you do not have to get approval from the narcissist in your life. Start to break away. A narcissist wants all attention, so they often isolate those they want to keep for themselves. This makes it easier for them to gain control over you. Spend time meeting new people or reconnecting with friends you might have lost touch with.

Seek out meaningful opportunities and activities. Consider going for that promotion you have wanted, volunteer, or try a new hobby. When you have a fulfilling life, its acts as a natural support system.

How to Treat a Narcissist

You want to start by distinguishing between a grandiose narcissist and a vulnerable one. When you are dealing with one that is vulnerable, they have a weak inner core they are masking with outward self-absorption and self-centeredness. The grandiose ones are not shy about how great they believe they are, and they truly believe they are the best.

Treating a narcissist in the right way is the easiest method to ensure that their negative behavior does not fall back on you and cause negativity in your life. To ensure that you are treating them in the right way, there are a number of things to do so you can evaluate them and develop the best strategy.

Determine the Narcissist's Type

You want to know if you are dealing with a vulnerable or grandiose narcissist. This makes it possible to determine what is needed to get the best response from them. For example, the grandiose type feels they are the best, so they need their ego stroked. On the other hand, the vulnerable type needs to feel special at all times due to their fragile ego. They need constant praise and reassurance.

Acknowledge How Annoyed You Are

Narcissists can really get into your skin, causing you to be annoyed with them. They want all of the attention, so they commonly interrupt you when you are doing anything other than giving them attention. Do not just blow this off. Instead, acknowledge that their behavior annoys you so you can start putting a stop to it.

Consider the Context

In many cases, certain situations trigger the worst narcissistic behavior. For example, you have a coworker who desperately wanted a promotion, but someone else got it. If she is a narcissist, this rejection may cause her to become very insecure, and in some cases, angry. This would result in her becoming spiteful, vindictive and downright difficult to deal with.

Know the Source of the Behavior

A narcissist does not think like everyone else. For those without narcissism, getting over insecurities is not overly difficult. It is just part of healthy coping. However, with a narcissist, they essentially need to have their ego rebuilt after a situation that caused them to feel inferior. It is important to balance how you treat them after a tough time.

For example, you are working on a school project with someone who is a narcissist. Something happens that exposes a weakness. This breaks their ego and can make them just stop working on the project, but you still need their contribution. To get them back on track, give them balanced reassurance. Too much and their ego can quickly get too big again, so approach the situation with this in mind.

Do Not Allow the Narcissist to Derail You

When you are doing something that takes attention away from them, they might try to sabotage you so that you stop doing it and get back to making them number one. It is important that you keep your goal upfront and do not allow anything they do or say to stop you from pursuing your goal or doing what you want to do.

For example, you and the narcissist usually do something together on Friday nights. However, you decide you want to start taking a class on your own. Since this takes your attention away from them, they may try to do things to get you to quit taking your class. Do not give in.

Make Sure to Stay Positive

Narcissists feed on watching other people feel bad, so even if they cause you to experience negative emotions, do not let them see this. When you are around them, make sure you are in a positive mindset. No matter how hard they try to bring you down, keep a smile on your face and do not react.

Call Their Bluff

Remember that the narcissist wants to keep you down because this makes it easier for them to control you. When they are trying to do something negative, do not give in and do not get offended. Instead, walk away or laugh. They want to see you upset, so if you do not do this in front of them, it starts to take away some of their control.

Know That They Need Help

Narcissism is a mental health issue that someone cannot just be willed away. They will need help if they ever expect to get their behavior under control. If you approach them and recommend they reach out to a professional, they are unlikely to agree and go. They may even become angry or defensive. If you care about the person and want them to at least consider help, approach the subject gently and know that this is something you will likely have to discuss several times before they will even consider it.

Freeing Yourself from Negative Emotions

Anger, jealousy, envy and other negative emotions can permeate your life and cause significant problems. It is important to recognize their existence and then work to be free of them. Freeing yourself from such emotions is a process, and it takes time. Even after you free yourself, you will need to commit to long-term work and maintenance.

Negative emotions are powerful and can quickly become habits if you do not get them under control. For example, if you commonly respond to criticism with anger, over time, this repetition will cause you to become angry any time you are criticized. This can start to impact your relationships, your career, and other elements of your life.

Stop Justifying

Stop justifying your negative emotions. If you are getting angry all of the time, take responsibility for why and stop trying to place the blame elsewhere. Anger is a very powerful emotion that can quickly become a habit. As soon as you recognize that this habit is problematic and admit it is not good, you can start to reevaluate why you are feeling this way so you can change it.

Stop Making Excuses

When you make excuses for negative emotions, either for yourself or others, you are telling yourself that they are out of your control. This is not true because you have the choice as to how you react to a situation. If you continue to make excuses, you will never take responsibility for your behavior. Over time, this can start to push people out of your life because they will not want to be around someone who cannot admit their faults or when they are wrong.

Take Responsibility

Once you dedicate yourself to no longer making excuses, you can start to take some responsibility for how you act in various situations. This starts by taking the power away from your negative emotions. As you continue to take responsibility, you will find that they lose their hold over you. The right reactions and choices will naturally start to become easier to make.

Do Not Overanalyze Other People's Opinions of You

Your emotions are your responsibility, but external factors can make them a bit harder to control. One of the biggest external factors is how other people view you. This is especially true if someone is especially vocal in criticizing you. This is often what narcissists do to keep you under their control.

Humans naturally want to be wanted and loved. When someone you respect or care about says something negative about you, the natural reaction is to go on the offensive. However, you want to instead hear what they are saying and then determine if it is true.

For example, did your supervisor yell at you for making a small error on a work project? Consider why they yelled. Think about the big picture. Okay, you made a small mistake, but overall, you completed the project and did well with it. Remember this and allow the yelling to roll off your back.

Stop Your Bad Habits

Any bad habit you have can add to the negatively in your life. For example, eating fast food often, smoking or not maintaining good dental hygiene. Take time to write down your bad habits. Once you put them in writing, they are easier to recognize. Start by working on one at a time because it is easier to correct a bad habit when you put a lot of focus on it. When you work to enhance your total wellbeing, your emotions will benefit.

Cut Off Negative People

If people in your life are largely a negative influence, walk away. It does not matter how close you are or how long you have known the person. When they are constantly negative, this is not doing any good for your life. If you really care about the person, you can consider talking to them. However, not everyone can change, and some may just not want to. For example, a narcissist is not able to just stop their negative behavior. It is a part of their personality. Because of this, simply talking to them is not likely to get you anywhere.

Think Before Responding

Negative emotions are powerful, so it is not uncommon for them to spill out. However, train yourself to wait 10 seconds before responding to a situation that causes negative emotions. This allows you to calm down so your response is appropriate for the situation. For example, you were supposed to meet a friend for dinner, and you were an hour late. They are upset. Instead of just responding back in anger and getting into a fight, count to 10 and then consider why they are mad. It will be easier to see that they did nothing wrong and you should apologize.

Be Grateful

Even during the worst of times, you have awesome things in your life that you should be grateful for. When you put your focus on them, it helps to alleviate the negative feelings. Consider keeping a journal and at the end of each day, take a few minutes to write down all the good things that happened that day. Over time, the positive elements of your life will start to naturally outweigh the negative.

Stop Saying, "I Can't"

If you keep telling yourself that you cannot do something, you will eventually start to believe it. This is what is referred to as a self-fulfilling prophecy. Give yourself credit and stop limiting yourself to what is easy and in your comfort zone. As you push yourself and see how many things you are truly good at, it will put you in a more positive frame of mind, naturally pushing out the negative emotions.

Let It Go

Life would be much simpler if everything could be controlled, but this is not possible. When you find something you have no control over, recognize it and let it go. For example, not every person will like you, and there are times when a loved one may get mad at you for something that is not your fault. Do not press the issue. Let go, and everything will eventually work itself out.

There are simple things you can start doing on a regular basis to push out negative emotions and enhance your overall wellbeing. You do not have to do every single one on a daily basis but consider them and incorporate some into your day when appropriate.

- Be proactive and do not allow the negative to settle into your life

- When life gets tough, cry it out because this aids in reducing stress

- Scream as loud as you can for a few seconds as this naturally counteracts negative emotions

- Get some sleep since it is easier to tackle stress and negative emotions when you are not exhausted

- Try to be positive and no matter what happens, force yourself to find the silver lining in the situation

- Take a few minutes to laugh every day since when you are laughing, negative emotions cannot be present

- Find someone you trust who cares about you and talk to them when you need to get help with a problem

- Consider an alternate perspective to see if it might allow you to better solve a problem

- Forgive yourself for setbacks as long as you recognize them and do not allow them to completely throw you off track

- Own your feelings and when negative emotions occur, recognize them, consider why you are experiencing them, and then detach from it

- Write about the day or experience you just had before going to bed each night as this allows you to leave the negative in the past so you can start fresh the next day

Chapter 6
Surviving Narcissistic Abuse

No matter how a relationship of this nature has put you down or worn you out, you can rise again. Despite the abuse and strife and all the mind games, you can come out strong and regain your sanity. Narcissism exists in different phases of life relationships. It is not only peculiar to romantic relationships; narcissism exists in business and at work, among families, siblings, and friends. But before we explore this, we should talk about the psychological effects of narcissism on its victims.

Impact of Narcissism on the Brain

Many people find themselves stuck in abusive relationships. It could be emotionally abusive parents, a friendship or romantic relationship. The effect is almost the same, which is more than mere emotional and physiological damage. Neuroscientists have revealed that narcissistic abuse can cause physical brain damage in victims.

When exposed to emotional trauma for an extended period, it can trigger symptoms of PTSD. This is why the remedy for abusive relationships is to leave. Walk away before you lose your entire self to this person. Unknown to many, the long-term effect of narcissism is way more than emotional and psychological distress.

What many do not know is that the brain is actually damaged by regular exposure to emotional abuse. With this prolonged exposure to abuse, the amygdala can swell and some experience a reduction in the size of the hippocampus (Morey, 2012.) The aftereffect of this is horrible, but to understand why, we must understand the role of the amygdala and hippocampus.

The amygdala is responsible for negative emotions such as fear, anxiety, worry, guilt, and shame. The hippocampus helps in the formation of memories as well as learning. To effectively learn as humans, we should be able to retain information into our short-term memory. This is the first step in learning. This needs to happen before any information gets transferred to long-term memory. In other words, short-term memory is as crucial to learning as long-term memory.

Damage to the hippocampus produces a devastating effect. According to a study at the University of New Orleans and Stanford University, a reduction of the hippocampus is linked to high levels of cortisol (a stress hormone) in the body (Carrion, 2007.) In other words, excess stress in people makes the hippocampus smaller.

The amygdala, known as the reptilian brain, is in charge of emotions such as fear, hate, lust, etc. It is also related to breathing and heart rate. It is responsible for triggering the fight and flight response. Victims of narcissistic abuse are always in a state where their amygdala is on high alert. With time, these people transition to a state where fear and anxiety become a constant, and the amygdala will pick up on the slightest sign of abuse.

Even after the victim has left the abusive relationship, there are lingering signs of post-traumatic stress such as panic attacks and excessive phobias. This is because the amygdala's increased size now considers the state of fear and anxiety as normal. To try and keep themselves from the reality of the situation, victims use reality twisting devices such as:

Projection: in a bid to try and deny the facts, victims choose to believe that the narcissist is not all bad. They want to believe deep down that there is some compassion. Most of the time, this is a lie.
Denial: victims refuse to accept the gravity of their situation. They convince themselves that living with it is better than any confrontation.
Compartmentalization: victims ignore the abusive aspects of the relationship and choose to focus only on the positive ones.

The Gradual Damage of the Hippocampus

The hippocampus helps us read, study, understand, and process information. In other words, the hippocampus handles everything related to learning and knowledge. Since it relates to learning, it is associated with the formation of new memories.

This crucial part of the brain is negatively affected by stress due to the presence of cortisol. Cortisol decreases the size of the hippocampus, making us more subjected to stress and anxiety. The more these distressing emotions thrive in the brain, the more our brain is changed.

Stress from narcissistic abuse, both of a short and long-term stress duration, are equally damaging. As a result, even subtle abuse and manipulation from the abuser can destroy the victim's brain. With many methods of healing available to those who experience abuse, you can reconfigure the brain to have a normal reaction to stress.

Surviving Narcissistic Abuse in Families

Do either of these scenarios sound familiar?

- A mother tells her daughter that no man will want her if she is fat
- A father lies to his children and dismisses their opinions, all to get them to do things for him

Some level of narcissism is prevalent in most families. There are many tactics a narcissist's parents could choose to exert control over their children. This often has a profound effect on the child, creating deep and painful wounds on the child's mental state. Being raised by a narcissistic parent can be devastating and potentially degenerating, causing low self-esteem if left unaddressed by the adult.

Naturally, it is believed that love should be instilled in all parents. There should be this unbroken bond that connects parents to their children. Looking specifically at the kind of intimacy a child shares with the mother, you expect to find an unbreakable chord of love that brings them together. However, not every mother is capable of unconditional love.

Some parents have been so eaten away by their past traumas that they don't see their children as special human beings deserving of their love. Instead, these parents only see them as extensions of themselves. This explains why they perceive their children as competition, a source of jealousy, and sometimes even a threat.

To narcissistic parents, their youngsters are objects that hinder their personal needs. Being raised by a narcissistic parent can be devastating for a child. However, healing is possible as soon as the child realizes it's important. You don't need to spend a lifetime trying to mend your broken and damaged self-esteem due to your parents. To heal, you have to:

Mourn: you were robbed of the normal childhood every kid deserves. Remember this and mourn properly as you would when losing something important.

Accept: you see another child's mother and wish yours was like her. You need to accept that your life is just different from others, and that's okay. Your upbringing has little to do with you; it was just an unfortunate turn to be born into a broken home, devoid of love and normal human emotions. You need to accept that this is who your parents were and make the best of it.

The process of grieving and accepting is primal to healing. This is not about healing the relationship with your parents but the relationship with yourself. Continuous exposure to abuse or neglect from your parents may have eroded your self-esteem, lowered your confidence, or made you feel unworthy of love, but there's always a chance to improve. The love, care, and attention you never received from your parents can instead come from you.

Other healing techniques are:

Get Rid of Your Inner Critic

During the abuse while with your parents, you believed they might love and accept you if you were more talented or smarter. When this never happened, you resolved that you were clearly unlovable. This left the voices of your parents in your head always criticizing and being negative. Allowing behavior like this to continue will only start a cycle of shame and abuse. Be kind to yourself and understand that no one is perfect.

Embrace Your Inner Child

You may think blocking it out is the way to cope. Nope. Think deeply about your feelings at this time. Look inward and see yourself when you were criticized and felt unloved. Embrace this helpless child and develop a strong, safe, loving relationship with that person - it is you after all. Rather than constantly criticizing yourself, try to see your flaws in a different way. With warmth and acceptance, embrace this poor damaged kid with compassion.

Exercise Self-Care

Living and growing up with narcissistic parents might have conditioned you not to focus on your needs. You only seek to please and do what you think makes them happy. As a result, you are completely lost on how to embrace your needs.

Fix this by treating yourself. Do something just for you and spend time alone to really begin to love for yourself, maybe an activity or adventure that makes you nothing but happy. You and your needs matter. Considering that a child spends an average of fifteen years living under the pressure of a parent, with narcissists, that time might feel like an eternity. Abuse doesn't happen overnight or over the span of a year, so the journey to recovery can be long and at times hard. Good things take time, so allow yourself to take the time you need while being surrounded by people you love. In time, you will see visible improvements in every aspect of your life; developing a healthy and loving relationship with yourself and others are just the baby steps you need to begin.

Healing Narcissistic Abuse in Relationships

Suffering mental, physical, and emotional abuse at the hands of a narcissist can be one of the most challenging things to get through. It affects every part of the victim's life, eroding their confidence and making them doubt themselves. Constant attacks with no relief or time for the mind and body to process the attack, let alone heal, is why many people end up with symptoms of PTSD.

The following steps can help the healing begin:

Create Ironclad Boundaries

To heal yourself from an abusive relationship, you need an imaginary barricade to keep the negativity out, in the form of boundaries. This is the foundation for your healing journey to get off the ground. Thinking you're out of the fray leaves you vulnerable to the narcissist, potentially giving them another chance to mess with your head. This contact can trigger pain that can pose as a major setback.

While the best method is to physically stay away from them, you can also give them the cold shoulder or just ignore them if getting away isn't easy. Leave no opportunity for them to prey on your emotions. Be emotionally distant even while interacting with them. You also need to learn object. This is a gradual way to build your self-esteem and regain your confidence.

Forgive Yourself

Some part of you knew all along that something was not right, but you were so drunk in love you didn't realize. This can make you shoulder the blame and be too hard on yourself. This won't help. Anybody could have been the victim, you were just in the right position to get in bed with a broken person. You were manipulated, tricked, and brainwashed. You could not have seen it coming even if there were a ton of warning signs. Realize that you are a whole person, full of love and deserving of love. You are kind, smart, and worthy. It is the narcissist's loss for not knowing your true worth.

Adjust Your Focus

Having spent a lot of time with your abuser, there will an overload of moments to reflect on. This is a trauma bond—a sign that there are unprocessed emotions you need to deal with. The idea here is to find time to work on them with mindful intention, rather than being dragged by your past forever. Embrace mindfulness and engage in visualizations of a bright and hopeful future.

The narcissist may have made you bench your dreams for theirs, but it's time for you to start working on them again. With a revitalized sense of purpose, you can get rid of the lingering thoughts of abuse that will hold you back.

Release the Abuser

The relationship with an abuser is often filled with anxiety and fear. You walk on eggshells anxious that the next thing you want to do will trigger their rage, causing a fight and a further unpleasant situation. There is a tendency for this to continue long after separation from the narcissist.

While we do not doubt the fact that narcissists love losing and can be stubborn in their pursuit, realize that they are not as strong as you think. They only want you to believe they are. With this in mind, the ability to get rid of the trauma bond will help you disarm them. You can now become established and resolute, unwavering even in the face of all their issues and drama.

Practice Mindfulness

When you stay sin an abusive relationship, you subconsciously transport yourself into a state of hyper-vigilance. You are always careful of your moves, afraid of doing anything to spook your abuser. This creates excessive stimulation of the sympathetic system, which leads to an influx of adrenaline and other stress chemicals into the blood.

The key to deactivate this is to activate the parasympathetic system. In other words, you are transitioning from fight or flight mode to rest mode. This comes from various methods such as deep breathing, mindfulness, or any activity that relaxes and eases your anxiety.

All in all, know that you can heal and break free from the shackles of an abusive relationship. Your effort to heal and recover yourself can be the ticket to a whole, integrated, and complete human being. You can improve!

Narcissism Among Friends

Friendship is a beautiful gift. You choose those that surround you, and these friends help make the world seem a little brighter and life worth living. Friends are there to catch us when we fall, and the people we are close to receive the investment of our trust and emotions. This bond can be overlooked by many, taking it for granted.

However, there are some instances where disturbing patterns, pain, and an unhealthy attachment seem to characterize the friendship. Some people are trapped in a narcissistic friendship without any idea of what that means, just that they are unhappy. Believing in someone's goodness is a basic premise of humanity. You hang on for the ride, longing for the friend you once knew to come back. Unfortunately, there are times when things can never go back.

Holding on too long can open you up to narcissistic abuse. Due to the attachment, our narcissist friend finds it easy to prey and impose on us. They see us as an extension of themselves, and nothing we ever do is good or acceptable. Worst of all, you never seem to agree on anything as your narcissist friend believes their opinions are more important, and right.

Rather than enjoying the benefit that comes from having a friend, the benefits of the relationship are one-sided. You are there to meet their needs and soothe their ego. Saying sorry is not in their dictionary, and they will never accept that they have done anything wrong. Holding on to this friendship for long starts taking its toll. By desperately trying to fix a broken friendship, we drown. Our self-worth, self-esteem and self-confidence will suffer for it.

The relationship becomes draining and you are exhausted, trying to salvage it.

Narcissism is real and plagues every facet of human relationships. Even though it is a lot to take in, many people find themselves in this kind of relationship. It is disappointing and shocking that such a thing could occur among friends, but that is the reality. If you have found yourself in this kind of relationship, here are some tips to keep your sanity intact:

Be Good to Yourself: you do not need another person to complete you. Any friend that takes advantage of you should be cut out of your life. Realize that friendship does not add value to you and is not worth the time.

Free Yourself: while there is nothing wrong with trying to help your friend, know when to draw the line. This might be difficult because letting go of a friend isn't always easy. But what friendship is worth the exhaustion?

Know What You Will Tolerate: narcissists, even in friendship, sees everyone as less than themselves. In their world, they are superior, so they expect to be treated like it. They also operate with the mindset that they can treat everyone like trash and a nobody. Know your self-worth and what you will not tolerate from your friend. Know when to draw the line.

Know When to Get Help: being in a narcissistic relationship is complicated and draining. It takes its toll on almost all areas of life. There are times you might need to seek outside help in order to recover from the anguish of dealing with a narcissist. There are support groups, and therapy can be of help.

<u>Knowing when to walk away</u> from a friend or relationship takes courage. It can be a lot to process, which hurts. However, you need to protect yourself from a friendship that drains the life out of you.

Workplace Narcissism

Narcissists are peculiar people, and they are easy to spot from an outsider's perspective. They occur in every facet of human interactions, including the workplace. They are typically obnoxious, overly outspoken and can make everyone around them uncomfortable. Using various manipulation techniques like mind control, they find it easy to get people entangled in their webs. As master manipulators, they can put up a front to get on the good side of people. They are charismatic, the life of the party, risk-takers, and they know how to get others to do things for them. This makes it easy for them to rise to a leadership position.

With narcissists, all that glitters is not gold. You need to know how to protect yourself from all their mind games and manipulations. We have the following tips to protect yourself from the narcissist

How to Spot a Narcissist

This is perhaps the most important part of surviving narcissism in the workplace. You need to keep yourself updated on the signs of a narcissist so you will not be caught in their traps. Narcissists are skilled at blending in to get what they want, and developing an ability to see past their veil will help. They might come off as friendly and charismatic at first. But as we have learned, they love making friends with people they can easily take advantage of.

They believe everything they do is under the radar so calling a narcissist out on their behavior might end up backfiring. They like to employ tactics like guilt, gaslighting, and criticism to create any type of chaos in their power, even in professional settings such as the workplace. Watch out for this.

Get Your Facts Right

If the narcissist your boss, confrontation might not be the best tactic. They are not against using dark tactics to confuse and disorient you, creating an unpleasant work situation and eventually getting rid of any threats.

Letting things go is not in their nature. With this in mind, you need to be smarter in your dealings with thing. Keep tabs on everything, all you observe, what they do and say. This will go a long way in protecting you and making a case for your arguments when the time comes.

Guard Your Weaknesses

Empaths and narcissists make for a toxic relationship because narcissists see the caring and nurturing nature of the empaths as a weakness. They see these as a loophole to get attached and entangled with them. If the empath knows their forgiving nature could get them into trouble, it's a good plan to keep this fact hidden.

In other words, a narcissist will draw near you if they feel there is something they can take advantage of. This calls for knowing yourself and the attributes that make you vulnerable. If you trust people easily, have trouble saying no and do things for people freely, the narcissist might explore these traits and use them to their advantage.

Avoid Taking Things Personally

In the world of narcissists, they are the most important person. They do not care about who gets hurt and who they victimize with their games. This is just how they are wired, and it is not your fault. It boils down to their need to put others down to feel better. With this in mind, do not feel sad or bitter if they make derogatory comments or try to belittle you. It's just their insecurity showing.

Throughout the book, we have made sure not to recommend confrontation with this type of personality as it can only end in more problems. You might not win if you call them out. Stroking their ego, while being a step ahead of them, is a good way to protect yourself. Keep these points in mind and know how to play your cards right.

Chapter 7
Helping a Narcissist Recover

You might wonder why we are talking about how you can help someone with narcissism when we have spent so long telling you that you can't fix them. That isn't the point. We're not suggesting that you can wave a magic wand and fix this person, allowing them to have meaningful and lasting relationships and friendships. We're suggesting that there are ways you can at least help someone, and maybe encourage them seek help.

Know right now that it might not work; narcissists are by their very nature very stubborn and are not going to accept help if they don't deem it to be strictly necessary. By suggesting that they may have a problem and need help, you are (in their eyes) attacking their very personality and self, and that will not be taken lightly.

Narcissists aren't always 100% narcissistic; you might have someone who only has narcissism when certain events trigger it, e.g. when they're rejected or go through a hard time, and as a result, their personality disorder comes to the fore. On the other hand, you might be dealing with someone who is narcissistic all the time, but not to a huge degree. These are the people you may be able to help, but for anyone who is 100% severe and toxic in terms of narcissism, don't even bother trying. These people will not take your suggestion well, and the only way that these types of narcissistic will ever receive help is when they take everything a step too far.

So, in what ways can you actually attempt to help a narcissist? There are very few ways, but you can try and encourage them to seek help by subtle moves. Again, this depends on the type of narcissism. You should also be very prepared for rejection, but know that at least you tried. From there, you can figure out your own options and decide what your own plan of action is going to be. Remember, you can't change someone else without their will; you can only control yourself.

There are three main ways you can attempt to help someone close to you who is clearly in the grips of NPD.

Do Not Allow Them to Manipulate You

This particular step is for you mainly, but it does help them indirectly. By refusing to let them manipulate you, and by allowing their gaslighting attempts to backfire, you're actually making them sit up and take notice. They will see that you are stronger, and they will wonder why. They will not want you to leave, as they need you around, even though their behavior probably shows otherwise.

In some ways, dealing with a narcissist is like dealing with a child.

If you tell them they can't have something, but then give in, they'll simply continue that level of behavior because they know you'll give in at some point. Narcissists will do the same thing, which is why it is so important that if you say you're going to walk out of the room when they belittle you, you actually do it. Do not apologize for something that isn't your fault and do not bow down to their demands. This will take practice, and it will be hard, but by looking after yourself and your own needs first, you will find the strength to do it.

By ensuring that their tactics backfire, you're taking away a huge amount of their power. This could go one of two ways : they could turn angry and simply lash out at your attempts, or they could possibly start to soften. It depends on the level of narcissism they are afflicted with. Of course, if they lash out, cut your losses and walk away. You've tried, and there's nothing more you can do.

Wait Until They are Calm, and Have a Discussion

If you've tried step one and it didn't go badly, e.g. they softened a little, then perhaps this second step will help. Remember that in order for someone to seek help, it has to be their decision. It's no good forcing someone to see a doctor if they don't believe anything is wrong with them. Think about an alcoholic, for instance. You can't force this person to admit they need help. The first step towards recovery is knowing there is a problem in the first place.

The types of treatment for NPD all hinge on a total commitment to the treatment at hand. If someone doesn't really believe they need help, the treatment isn't going to work at all. So, the point of this step is to simply sow a seed in their mind and help them explore the possibilities.

Wait until they are calm to sit down and have a conversation. Be soft and don't be forceful. Talk to them, not at them, and make sure that you keep your emotions on an even keel. Tell them that you feel like they're treating you in an unfair way and give examples to back up your words. Tell them that you know they don't mean to treat you this way and they are a good person. If they remain calm, you may be able to make progress. If they simply throw a narcissistic tantrum and turn it around, again, you can't do anymore.

Find some literature on NPD and leave it on the table. Tell them that you've found this information and perhaps they might like to read it. Suggest you read it together, or they can read it on their own, and you'll be by their side whatever they decide.

Remember, it's not 100% guaranteed that this step will work, but it's worth a try if you want to know you did all you could before you decide to walk away. It's also important that by some stroke of luck, they agree to perhaps talk about things over with a health professional, and they recognize there might be something not quite right. Then you remain supportive and on their side at all times. Remember that deep down, a narcissistic is lacking in confidence and needs constant reassurance. The fact that you've suggested there might be something wrong could go either way, but by being calm and supportive - being on their side at all times - you may be able to guide them through it and toward professional help.

Issue an Ultimatum

This is the final method to try, and it's not one you should attempt as the first port of call. This is not likely to go well, but there is a chance. By issuing an ultimatum, you're basically saying, "look, I do not want to be treated in this way, but I know it's now what you really mean to do deep down. I'm giving you one chance to sort this out, and I will be by your side all the way. If you refuse, and if you continue to act in this way, I will leave for good."

You have to go through with your ultimatum and do not attempt to go back on it. Be strong and see it through, whatever way it goes. The point of this, however, is not to shout and lecture, it's a firm statement of intent. If you add emotions and hysterics, they are not going to take you seriously.

These are the only ways you can attempt to help someone with NPD, without actually being a health professional. Even if you were a health professional, the person would need to be willing to seek help and make a commitment to really putting in the effort to change. Treatment for NPD is quite intensive and requires a lot of deep thinking and behavioral change. It requires a strong will to make it work, so you can see why someone being forced to seek help is not going to have a good outcome.

The Importance of Knowing You Cannot "Save" Anyone

We've said this once, and we need to say it again. You cannot "save" a person with NPD, and you cannot fix them. This intention can only come from themselves. It's sad to walk away from someone who has a condition and doesn't actually "mean" to act in a certain way, but at the same time, you can't wave a magic wand and make it all go away again either.

The only thing you can do is focus on yourself and go with what you feel is right. You know in your gut that you deserve happiness and if your partner/friend or whoever this person is to you is not going to give you that, the only thing you can do for yourself is walk away. If you are in a relationship with this person, what would happen if children come into the equation? Would you want them to be born into a relationship with a large narcissistic element? That is certainly something to think about.

Make sure you have this fact in your mind before you attempt to help someone with NPD and before you make a decision to walk away. By knowing that in a solid and firm manner, you won't have regrets about your final actions.

Highly narcissistic people are usually unaware that they are so as they live very often in a state of denial and are unlikely to attempt to improve or work on themselves.

The Future for a Narcissist Who Refuses Help

It doesn't paint a great picture if the person isn't willing to seek help. In that case, it's far more likely that the narcissist will end up jumping from destructive relationship to destructive relationship, and if they do end up in a long-term union, it's unlikely that their partner will be truly happy and fulfilled. That person is far more likely to be simply "putting up" with the narcissism.

If a narcissist ends up in a relationship that yields children, the sad truth is that their children are quite likely to develop narcissistic tendencies as a result during their early years. While there isn't a certain answer to what causes NPD, there a definite suggestion that childhood experiences create a firm link to the personality in their adolescent and then adult years.

Narcissists also have the habit of becoming quite bitter over time. This is partly because people have come into their lives and left them, and they can't see why. Of course, they will project the blame onto the other person and don't see their role in them leaving. Many narcissistic traits, therefore, worsen with age, as more experiences are racked up throughout life.

As you can see, it's quite a bleak picture we're painting. and that is the sad truth about life as a narcissist. People can only stand being treated a certain way for so long before they eventually pluck up the courage to leave. While some never get to that point, these relationships are likely to be empty and lacking in true love and respect. For these reasons, the biggest price a narcissist pays for their actions over time is loneliness and a lack of a truly meaningful relationships in the end. For a narcissistic, however, the most loving and deep relationship they have is with themselves.

Chapter 8
The Narcissist and Empathy

When it's Time to Leave

At this point, your partner must be willing to at least try to make some changes in their behavior to improve their own mental health and the relationship. If your partner is willing to do some of the work, then your relationship can be saved. But, if you have been engaging in the activities discussed previously in this book, and your partner still does not see any problem with their behavior, there isn't much hope for an improvement.

Unfortunately, as much as we want to believe that we can change another person, we cannot always do so. You can change the dynamics on your end, which can improve the relationship for you, but in order for your partner to truly overcome their narcissistic traits, they have to put in some effort on their own. This chapter will outline some of the things that your partner can do to improve their narcissistic tendencies. These techniques are the last step to turn a narcissist into a loving and attentive partner.

Identify the Maladaptive Behaviors that Need to be Changed

What types of behaviors does your partner see as maladaptive or problematic? This could come from a list that you make or your partner understands to be true, or a combination of both. Once your partner acknowledges the inappropriate behaviors, he or she can begin to attack and alter them head on.

Once you both know and understand the types of behaviors to work on, you can set up a positive and negative reinforcement system. Basically, if your partner does something positive to change their behavior, they should be rewarded somehow, and if they engage in one of the behaviors you are trying to get rid of, a form of negative reinforcement (often called punishment) should be used like the "No Contact" principle. It works when, for instance, your partner gets abusive, and you distance yourself from him or her to protect yourself and cool things off. Your partner will eventually realize his or her mistake and will ask you to deal with the problem.

The punishments and rewards should be worked out between you both, and your partner has to be willing to commit to them. Many studies have shown that positive reinforcement works better than negative long term, so it makes sense to reward all small behaviors. If these rewards involve both of you, it could be a great way to strengthen your bond.

Practice Service to Others

People can learn to care for others. They have to choose to put the needs of another person before their own needs. If your narcissistic partner is willing to try this, it will be the first step to a more loving partnership. To do so, your partner should put aside one of their needs and do something for you no matter how simple or small. Whether it means running an errand that you usually do, making dinner, or taking care of one small thing so you don't have to, ask your partner to do something just for you. Start with something small, and over time, your partner will develop the ability to do more and more.

If your partner is willing to do these things for you, it is a good sign that they are willing to change. Talking about each other's needs and deciding the boundaries on both sides of the relationship is important. If your partner is amenable to do things for you, you, yourself, should be ready to do things for them as well, especially with regard to their mental health and stability. As discussed earlier, you have the right to say no to unreasonable demands, but, in a loving relationship, you have to give as well. But it must be reasonable.

Your partner will learn that providing a service to others will benefit both of you, and your partner will experience personal joy from seeing you happy, but it takes practice. Service to others is important to develop empathy for another person, which is the next step in the process.

Practice Empathy

Simply defined, empathy is the ability to put yourself in another person's place. By imagining how another person feels, you can relate to them better. The narcissist needs to do this, and it is a skill that takes practice. You can facilitate this by explaining to your partner how you feel when they do a certain thing. As they begin to understand this, they will be better able to put themselves in the position of another. Once your partner can understand how another person feels, they will be more likely to help them.

Don't Take Life so Seriously

To someone with narcissism, not getting their way seems like a life and death situation. But examining what happens if the narcissist doesn't get their way makes it easier to understand that horrible things will most likely not happen. The narcissist needs to remind themselves that they are not perfect, and they do not have to be. They need to look for the humor in little things. As soon as they learn not to take life so seriously, humor can be found. And tomorrow, it probably won't even be that important.

Once your partner realizes that even though yesterday seemed like a life and death situation, it's not the same as the present situation, and it will become easier to laugh at their own mistakes and move forward in a more loving way. When everything is no longer about them and they face the fact that they cannot get everything they want and learn that it is not a crisis, things will get easier. They will learn to let go of things and move on more easily. Your partner will learn that they do not have to have control of everything and that life will not fall apart.

Practice Self-Compassion

If your narcissist is the grandiose type, it is all the more important to practice self-compassion rather than develop self-esteem. Your narcissistic partner already has plenty of confidence, and this is what makes them think they are entitled to everything they want and desire. Instead, fostering self-compassion will help promote tenderness for other people. And, in the end, what will cause your partner to change their behavior is understanding that everyone deserves love and respect. It starts with loving and respecting themselves.

To foster self-compassion, consider the three steps: developing self-kindness, understanding our common humanity, and practicing mindfulness.

Self-kindness is the simple idea that we should not beat ourselves up when something goes wrong. It means that when we talk to ourselves in our mind, it should be kind, rather than harsh. If you or your partner makes a mistake, what thoughts go through your mind? Do you berate yourself or do you try to comfort yourself? Most narcissists will berate themselves and then lash out to try and make they feel better. Instead of lashing out at themselves, they should practice saying kind things in their mind. Remind yourself that everyone makes mistakes and it's okay not to be perfect because no one is. Say nice things to yourself.

Second, realizing that everyone faces the same struggles will help to connect to that common bond we call humanity. Everyone has imperfections. Everyone feels insecure at times, and everyone has problems. When you practice self-compassion, you put yourself on the same level with everyone else around you. This is a necessary step for the narcissist. When they are able to do this, they can stop treating everyone else as if they are only meant to serve their needs. They will realize that they are part of a greater whole, not above it. This will make it easier for them to change their behaviors. This is a key realization to turn a narcissist into a loving human being: that everyone comes from the same place and has issues from various roots. No one's problems or ideas are more important than another's.

Lastly, the narcissist must learn to practice mindfulness which means keeping their thoughts in the present moment. It also means acknowledging their feelings as they happen and thus dealing immediately with them. Suppressing what one thinks and feels causes emotional outbursts later. By dealing with them in the present moment, the narcissist will be less likely to act out in negative ways.

By working through these steps, the narcissist can be turned into a thoughtful and loving person. Self-compassion, when practiced regularly, will naturally transform into compassion for the world around them. It will need much effort and will take time. Doing these things is not an easy, but the benefits for both the narcissist, and you, as the partner, will be immensely gratifying.

Understanding Gas Lighting

Gas lighting comes from the movie of the same name that was released in 1944. It refers to a manipulation tactic some people use, especially the narcissist, to try and cause doubt in the minds of their victims. The way a person gaslights depends on the situation, but the main objective remains the same. They want to re-invent past events to make sure their errors or mistakes stay hidden.

In the example above, Margaret clearly remembers that her mother spanked her and her siblings. This was verified by the conversation she had with her brother, so she knew she hadn't made it up. When her mother noticed how good her granddaughter acted, she knew that Margaret's parenting was working, which showed her choice of spanking wasn't the best discipline method. With this in mind, Margaret's mother wanted to create distance between her and that discipline practice since it has become seen as harmful, ineffective, and unnecessary. She chose to claim she never did it, despite the fact Margaret and her brother remember having to face it as children.

With this example, the gas lighting seems relatively harmless and Margaret could just brush it off. But with narcissistic gas lighting, it becomes extreme, and it can create serious doubt and even cause their victim to start questioning their sanity. This is only one tactic that a narcissist will use to protect their image, not just how they appear in the present, but in the past as well. They have to make sure that they appear correct in every part of their life, so they strive to stay away from being branded for little mistakes even if they took place decades ago. Gas lighting allows them to sweep these mistakes under the rug while also hurting a person's sanity, which to them, means nothing.

Smear Tactic

If you start to notice that people distance themselves from you once you get out of the clutches of the narcissist, they have probably started a smear campaign. While politics typically holds the most popular smear campaigns, narcissists will sometimes use these same strategies. Once you cut ties with a narcissist, they have realized something: you know who they truly are. This means that if you were to start exposing the narcissist for whom they really are, which likely isn't even a part of your plan, then they are going to have to be carefully because their façade may start to crumble. This isn't something that they want to face.

What is a narcissist to do? They will use smear campaigns to stay a step ahead of the game. They use the information they have about you and the relationship you had. They will make sure to talk with mutual friends before you do to clarify the reasons why you two are no longer speaking. This will likely involve tweaking some information to make you out to be the bad guy.

It's important to note that a narcissist is not going to settle for just mentioning a couple of nasty things. They are looking to completely destroy your reputation and credibility. This ensures that you will have a very hard time convincing your friends what you really experienced. You will come off as unreliable, and they keep the friends and their reputation.

If the narcissist chooses to do a smear campaign, it can leave you without anyone to turn to. Some gossip and rumors can be so bad that it harms your job and other relationships. Keep in mind that they never really cared about you to begin with, so don't be surprised if they become somebody unrecognizable and start sharing absolute lies about you and the things you have done.

Abuse by Surrogate

The one thing that a narcissist never runs out of is people. People gravitate towards them for the same reason you did. Unfortunately, if somebody chooses to cross a narcissist, they will find themselves dealing with attacks from the rest of their posse.

This is something that you could refer to as abuse by surrogate, and it will start the moment you upset them. Their need to discourage and shame will hit full force, and they are going to make sure that you feel their unhappiness for what you have done to them. They will also take things a step further and hit where it hurts. This is where other people will step in.

Narcissists, as discussed above, will start to talk to other people in their circle about you. They will convince them that you are the one at fault, and you must be taught a lesson. The interesting thing is that they won't actually say those exact words. It looks more like brainwashing when making other people believe certain lies and encouraging them to act on certain ideas without instruction.

Here's an example: Damito is the middle child. Her sisters are A+ students and they bring home impeccable report cards and get a lot of praise from their teachers. Damito is just an average student. While she may not get the grades her siblings do, she does come home with decent grades. She is by no means failing. One day, though, she fails an exam and her mother loses her mind. She reprimands her, says she's lazy and that she is worried about her future. She says that her performance isn't going to get her anywhere in life, and it upsets her to say that Damito isn't going to achieve what her sisters will.

Damito is sent to her room after being reprimanded in front of the family at dinner. She cries and sulks in her room for the rest of the night. Meanwhile, her sisters are still at the dinner table, and her mother continues to complain. She praises Damito's sisters. The great grades give meaning to the long hours she spends at work to afford their schooling. The children feel happy and loved by their mother's words, and they thank her for all of the effort she has put in to make sure that they can get the best education.

While they are talking, she calls Damito ungrateful, saying she doesn't deserve to get the same opportunities as her sisters because she doesn't appreciate what her mother does. She goes on to tell them that they shouldn't associate with people like Damito because they can be bad influences and cause them to lose sight of the things that are important. Before their conversation comes to an end, she says that she still has to work hard and hopes for the best, even if some of them don't appreciate what she does. The end their conversation and the kids go to bed.

The following day, Damito gets up and heads to the kitchen for breakfast to find that all of the food has been eaten. "You got up late, so you don't get food," her older sister tells her rudely. During the day Damito is showered with the same harsh and negative energy from her sisters who seem to be avoiding her.

This makes her feel ashamed and alone. This causes her to approach her mother and apologize for being ungrateful for all of the work she has done. Her mother "accepts" her daughter's apology, but she stays cold towards her daughter in the next few days, which her sisters mimic. Can you see the problem in this scenario?

First, it's important to see the reason for the aggravation. What did Damito do to get this kind of treatment from her mother and then her sisters? A single failed test. For the majority of us, one bad grade isn't a reason to get this upset. In fact, most parents would let this slide with saying more than, "do better next time."

However, since Damito's mother is a narcissist, she views any type of failure as completely unacceptable. Her children are an extension of her, so if they have any shortcomings, it is completely unforgivable because if reflects badly on her. She made a point of reprimanding Damito in front of her sisters. This shows her anger and imparts shame because everybody else gets to hear and see her receiving this punishment.

Next, once Damito leaves, and her mother continues to talk with her sisters. She starts out by praising them, telling them how proud she is of them being top students. Of course, it's easy to infer that they only perform well because of the pressure from their mother and not because they actually want to do well. By talking to Damito's sisters, she can trick them into feeling the same animosity towards Damito, who didn't even do anything malicious to anybody in the family.

Her sisters and her mother don't have a real reason to be upset with her because the grade she gets doesn't affect any of them. However, since her mother used the tactic of divide and conquer, they feel connected to her and thus become aligned by mimicking how she feels. What happens next? They unknowingly emotionally abuse Damito by giving her the cold shoulder. They distance themselves and treat her like a pariah. This causes Damito to feel the brunt of her "mistake" and she has no choice but to apologize, even though she shouldn't have to.

Abuse by surrogate can be hard to handle because it causes the victim to feel isolated. They start questioning themselves and may even begin to believe their abuser had a good reason to treat them so badly. What's more, they feel the added pressure from the "mob" which complicates their internal battle. If everybody is mad at me, then I must have done something wrong.

What is important to remember here is that just because several people believe something doesn't make it true. When you are at the brunt end of abuse by surrogate, it can cause you to start questioning your validity and integrity, but you stay strong and decide to believe that the truth will help you to be less affected by their abuse and disapproval.

Dealing with Emotional Abuse

If you or your partner find these steps quite difficult, it can be useful to seek professional help. A therapist or counselor can be an impartial guide in following these steps and can provide essential insight that you both missed. They can make sure that the two of you are not seeking to hurt each other, even unintentionally. Although not necessary, a therapist can be a valuable asset in the quest of turning your narcissist partner into an unselfish, loving partner.

It is my sincere hope that you and your partner are both willing to put the work necessary into your relationship to improve it. By following the techniques laid out in this book, you will have the person you love turn into a thoughtful, unselfish partner. But they, too, have to be willing to do the work. Remember, you cannot force someone to change. You can change how you act, but if your partner is not willing to engage in the work laid out in this chapter, there is only so much you can do to improve your relationship. But, working together, you and your partner can accomplish miraculous things. You can get the loving partner you want while and he or she learns to deal with life and relationships more effectively.

Chapter 9
Healing from Narcissistic Abuse

To the people reading this who have survived narcissistic abuse, good for you. Now it is time for the healing to begin. The good news is that there are many approaches you can take to get your life back in order. In applying the various healing techniques, be sure to give yourself time. The abuse did not occur overnight, and neither will your reparations. With these thoughts in mind, here are the recommended healing techniques to revitalize your life after narcissistic abuse.

Meditation

Meditation is a great way to center yourself through active body movement and deep breathing. Healing narcissist abuse brings victims face to face with their source of fear. The memories and images of past abuse that may have been buried will likely be brought to light once you quiet your mind. The intention of this practice is to help you embrace your past experiences, good or bad, while disarming the traumatic effect the bad thoughts have had on you.

Studies have established that meditation can help combat symptoms of PTSD (Cohut, 2019). Meditation reduces the stress hormones by soothing our sympathetic nervous system, which triggers the fight or flight hormones. We have included the following tips to help with peaceful meditation specifically dealing with trauma.

Find a Safe Place to Meditate

After leaving the abuser and ending the toxic relationship, there is a tendency to have flashbacks that trigger panic attacks. The presence of your abuser matters as it reinforces the attacks.
For meditation to be effective, you must feel safe. This feeling of peace must sink into your subconscious so that you relax and feel unencumbered. Find a quiet spot where you are alone, lay out a mat, maybe light some candles. Put on meditation music or "ohm" in a low tone to keep distractions at bay. Breathe, as this is the beginning of healing.

Find Other Ways to Meditate

There are many approaches to mindfulness. In fact, should you develop panic attack or anxiety, doing something, anything, to keep yourself distracted can help. It can be while washing the dishes. With every stroke of the sponge, you can drift into a state of mindfulness. It could be while mowing the lawn, brushing your teeth, etc. All you are to do is focus your thoughts on the task at hand. With this, you are not actively attempting to meditate but to complete your chores.

Be a Witness to Your Flashbacks

It is common for victims of abuse to have physical reactions to any thoughts of their abuse or abuser. With meditation, you can witness your thoughts in a controlled setting rather than reacting to them. While reliving the memories of your abuse, it does not have to paralyze you as it did before. With meditation, you can be a gentle observer of the memories of your abuse. This way, you can strengthen your control which will lead to a significant improvement over time.

Group Therapy for Healing

Group therapy involves the coming together of people in similar situations who have experienced narcissistic abuse. These share their struggles and how they were overcome. This allows victims to come to terms with the fact that they are not alone. Group therapy exposes victims to various approaches through which they can heal. Group therapy offers patience, courage, and strength to heal, recover, and eventually get your mental health in order. It can help tap into the inner strength needed to live a healthy and satisfying life.

A Typical Group Therapy Session

Group therapy is handled by a trained therapist and the sessions consist of six to twelve members all sharing their stories. The idea is for people with similar characteristics (in this case, victims of a narcissist's abuse) to voice their concerns, experiences, and coping strategies in a safe environment. Group therapy works best in combination with meditation and other forms of therapy.

The idea of sharing your nightmares in a room full of strangers might be scary, but it has a wide range of benefits. With the diversity that exists within a group, the victims of narcissistic abuse can develop new and healthy strategies. Hearing others share their tale of abuse can do a lot for your journey.

Types of Group Therapy

Most group therapy occurs in two forms: process-oriented group therapy and psycho-educational group therapy. In the process-oriented group experience, the therapist does not take a major role. They only act as a moderator and encourage members to share. This creates a sense of belonging in each member and a feeling that they are in charge of the session. This is the type of group therapy that best helps victims of narcissistic abuse.

The psycho-educational group experience, on the other hand, puts the therapist in charge. He teaches members healthy and scientifically-tested coping skills to solve various life problems. The therapist is the center of attention here as they play the role of teacher.

Cognitive Behavioral Therapy for Narcissistic Abuse Recovery

Over the years, CBT has proven to be pretty effective in helping trauma victims. The aim is to bring improvement by systematically changing patterns of thoughts, feelings, and behaviors. CBT revolves around the fact that the three are connected and an improvement in one can trigger an improvement in another.

With CBT, patients can learn:
- Helpful coping mechanisms for stress and how to handle trauma
- To interact with their trauma in a new way that does not trigger a negative reaction
- How to develop an objective understanding of their relationship with the narcissist to help revive their sense of control and also develop healthy coping skills.

The therapist helps victims to reconsider their thinking patterns to detect unhelpful patterns. These are the patterns that might have occurred due to continuous exposure to the abuse. For instance, victims might think they are bad people for attracting a narcissist. Unbeknownst to them, narcissists do not take an interest in weak or insignificant people. They prefer to go for strong and powerful people who can soothe their egos, people they can exploit. Victims, however, do not know this. With this therapy, victims begin to see themselves in a new light. The aim is to help bring the traumatic experience to a new light. This way, they get a new perspective about the incidence as well as their ability to cope.

Many times, victims of narcissistic abuse avoid and suppress memories of the abuse or anything that triggers their time with the abuser. CBT can help reduce this by assisting patients in embracing the occurrence in a healthy way. This involves a planned and controlled exposure in a way and at a pace that the patient is comfortable with. This bring control and confidence, rather than resorting to avoidance behaviors.

Yoga for Narcissistic Abuse Healing

Over the years, yoga has grown in popularity as a means of connecting the mind and body. As a mindfulness exercise that uses various breathing and relaxation techniques combined with physical movement, yoga has proven to successfully treat mental health issues as well as trauma from past occurrences.

Continuous exposure to stress and potentially life-threatening situations reconfigures the body into fight-or-flight mode. Even though this is the body's way of saving us from danger, excessive stress raises the cortisol level that we know triggers mental health problems.

Yoga has a soothing effect on all levels of stress in the body. It can calm the body and transport it to a state of tranquility. A common factor with victims of trauma is the inability to adequately process and heal from their experiences. This is why traditional therapy alone is not very helpful.

Introducing Trauma-Sensitive Yoga

Trauma-based yoga stands out in that it directs the body awareness of the present moment to take care of any symptoms arising from abuse or trauma. This emphasizes the internal experiences of the victim who is intending to get in touch with their body at the present moment.

These helpful feelings could be anything from how the cloth hugs their body to the movement of air through their lungs. The aim is exposing how they can take action about their experience. With this yoga practice, students can learn to get in touch with their bodies and minds.

Yoga, in combination with psychotherapy, can help reduce the after effects of trauma and narcissistic abuse while reinforcing positive emotions such as acceptance, compassion, and empowerment.

Self-Hypnosis for Healing

Hypnosis is a way to reach memories that are out of one's consciousness. Self-hypnosis tries to provide a positive restructuring to dissociated traumatic memories. In other words, with self-hypnosis, victims can face their fears and the traumatic time spent with the narcissist. Rather than being hindered by the memory, patients embrace these memories in a new dimension. This is done with the aim of re-moralizing memories like self-protection and at times, pity for the abuser.

With this, victims can access the traumatic memory in a controlled way while viewing them from a broader perspective. There are many forms of self-hypnosis, but we will run through the eye fixation self-hypnosis method in this book. Be sure you are in a quiet room without distractions. Get into a comfortable position and make sure you are well seated without crossing your legs and feet. Your clothes should not be too tight, and we suggest no shoes.

Look up and take a deep breath. Pick a point on the ceiling and direct your gaze, without straining your neck. With your gaze fixed in this position, breathing in deeply, pause, and exhale. Repeat this for sometimes and relax. Close your eyes and feel every tension in your body drift out. Allow Your Body to Relax. Let go of all tension in your body and sit in a relaxed position. Countdown from five and let your body relax deeper with every count.

Direct your attention to your breath, note the rising and falling of your chest. The key is not in trying to relax your body. Rather, it is in allowing your body to relax.

Bring Back Your Consciousness

Count from one to five and open your eyes. Open your eyes at the count of five, stretch your arms and legs

You might not feel as calm as you would want. The key is growing with practice as there is a learning curve.

Using EMDR to Heal Narcissistic Abuse

With Eye Movement Desensitization and Reprocessing (EMDR), victims can unlock past hurtful experiences. It is not a traditional therapy and works best over a few sessions. It has healing effects on the thoughts, feelings, and memories of the past, and in this case, narcissistic abuse.

EMDR is an intense form of therapy in that it seeks to unlock painful memories, associated with the abuser. It is a psychotherapy that helps people heal and recover from the emotional distress of a traumatic event.

Humans generally have either the left or right brain hemisphere dominant. However, EMDR with bilateral stimulation helps activate both sides. Since they both work at the same speed and capacity, there is rapid processing. This reconfiguration makes it easy to identify trauma by highlighting the affected area. Rather than the trauma being stuck, it gets processed in a healthy manner.

Many victims of abuse, specifically narcissistic abuse, react to the memory of the trauma like it just happened. Part of the aim of EMDR is to curtail this. For instance, you remember how your abusive partner yells at you. Nothing you did was good enough which made you sad and angry. The difference now is that even though you remember every detail; you do not feel the anger.

This is what EMDR is trying to achieve. It helps reprocess the memory such that even if you remember how hurtful the experience of the abuse was, you no longer feel the physical manifestation. Not only do you have a renewed approach to these memories, but you also have to let go of the hatred and resentment you had for your partner.

Chapter 10
Dating After Leaving a Narcissist

Getting back control of your life after years of abuse might seem like a difficult thing to do. But with the right guidance and using the right tools, you can effectively regain your control and find happiness again.

Get the Negativity Out of Your System

Like it or not, there is a whole lot of negativity within your system by the time you are parting with a narcissist. This toxicity accumulated as you tried to appease them and in trying to make the relationship work. You tried to understand the narcissist as they took advantage of you more and more. It is now time to let go of all that darkness and allow space for your life to take shape again.

Some of the things you can do to get this negativity out include journaling or sharing your story with a friend, or even engaging a therapist. Talking out the story is so helpful, especially when it is with a listening partner since it helps in organizing your confused thoughts into place. Also, it helps to empower you since you can finally be honest with yourself. You can engage in mind and body exercises such as yoga or dancing that help to discard the toxicity and clears your mind to accommodate positivity.

Compile a List of the Controlling Incidents you Have Experienced

Although this might seem trivial, compiling the experiences of control and abuse helps you realize what you have been through and appreciate your growth - the fact that you will not allow yourself to be in such a situation again. Such remembrance gives you pride in your bravery in leaving and looking forward to a more rewarding life. You appreciate that you can now live as a free person and cannot allow yourself to fall back in the abusive relationship.

Practice Listening to Your Inner Self

Your inner voice is the best tool you will ever have in dealing with any situation. It shows you how best you can do things and it never lies. Even amid great pain and desperation, your inner voice will show you how to find your way out. The major reason why the narcissist was able to manipulate you was that they worked on the external stimulants of your brain, which in turn messed your internal stimulants as argued by Morf, Horvath and Torchetti (2011). They were fulfilling their selfish motives by controlling how your brain responds to things. However, listening to your inner voice will help you review a situation and you can learn when to move ahead, hold back, or reject the things being said to you. It will guide you in your newly acquired life, one in which you are free. Now you understand yourself much better and will never fall for a toxic person again.

Organizing Time and Space

It is good to have a clean and organized space since this allows you enough time to absorb everything that comes your way. When your space is full of clutter, you feel overwhelmed because it registers in your mind that you have a lot to do. Decluttering allows you to organize your space and keep only the things that matter to you. You will find that your brain will respond positively to living in an ordered place. You will feel more settled and you are energized to face every new day. Also, clutter obscures your mind and your thinking. You can establish a good daily routine where your most significant tasks are allocated to the time of the day you tend to be most active.

Connect with Family and Friends

As noted, narcissists usually isolate their victims from their loved ones and friends. They no longer understand you, and they may even think that you hate them. They have judged you countless times because your attitude towards them has changed. Some of them could have tried to tell you that you are not okay in your relationship, but you have always denied their sentiments in an attempt to defend your narcissist partner, who had already conditioned you to support them against all forms of attack. Since you have been dependent on the narcissist for all your social contact needs, you find it difficult to associate with people. The truth is, however, that your loved ones are always eager to reconnect and spend time with you.

Be Patient: Take Your Time

The worst mistake you can commit is to judge yourself and think you are not making fast progress regarding getting out of the pit and forgetting your narcissist. You should not be hard on yourself. Instead, understand that healing takes time to be effective. Also, everyone needs different amounts of time to get over something. Based on the depth of your abuse or length of the toxic relationship, you might need more or less time to heal.

There is no time limit on healing. Remember, your abuser has already separated you from your most precious people and hobbies. They conditioned you into feeling lost and lonely without them. Therefore, healing might take time, and it is upon you to be kind to yourself and patient as you heal. Most importantly, do not jump right into another relationship. This will obscure your thinking and deny you time to heal. Consequently, you will carry the burden right into the next relationship, and it will not be healthy.

Acknowledge What has Been and Forgive Yourself

You might be tempted to beat yourself up for allowing such a toxic person in your life for such a long time. However, true healing and regaining power entails accepting that you have associated yourself with a highly toxic person, who has consciously hurt you. Accept that you have been tricked and abused. Trying to please them and showing them that you understood them denied you the chance to identify the red flags. Also, they used your strengths against you: you were caring, you had a good job, you were highly organized, open to new ideas, and financially stable. You never deserved this, and it was wrong of them to abuse you.

After acknowledging this, know that it was not your fault and forgive yourself. Forgiving yourself is the most important thing you need to do right now. No matter how much time, energy, wellness, and cash you have lost, that is all in the past. You have to forgive yourself and move forward. It does not matter why you stayed for so long, but it does not matter why you were fooled. But it already happened. So, forgive yourself.

Seek to Acquire Knowledge: do Self-Inquiry

It seems so difficult to make sense of the abuse you have been through and what to do after this. For such a long time you have only learned to see the world through the perspective of your abuser. You are now confused and are wondering where to begin. Seek to be knowledgeable about emotional wellness. There are a myriad of articles and online courses you have access to that can help you.

Knowledge is power, and enhancing your power never goes out of fashion.

Shift Your Focus

Because you have been abused for a long period it is easy to find your mind moving back to these thoughts. These are aspects of trauma and cognitive dissonance and are a hindrance to proper recovery. The reason why your mind keeps on pushing you back there is that it wants to comprehend certain things and process related emotions.

You should not entertain these thoughts about the past but capitalize on the present. You may find yourself taking one step forward and two steps backward. Train your mind to be in the present and the future you have chosen to make for yourself. To boost your motivation in this endeavor, you need to resurrect your dreams - and this time let them be magnificent. Remember the dreams and things you wanted for yourself before being drawn to the narcissist; think about how bad you wanted them and boost your desire to achieve them. This is what it means to shift your focus to looking forward and changing your status from that of a victim to a hero in your life. Even though you have been through pain, after healing you may be surprised by the self-loving person - aware, whole, and integrated - you have become.

Chapter 11
Case Study and its Implications

We will now take the case study of a patient called Diana, who visited an individual therapist. This is what was gathered from the therapist's point of view. Diana was raised by a narcissist mother who blamed her for almost everything. The mother would be aggressive to Diana; then, she would tell her poor daughter that it was her fault that her mother treated her that way. Diana grew up with low self-esteem. She became a target for a narcissist partner and fell for him. Finally, she was mistreated, abused, and left in trauma. Luckily she decided to seek help. In the therapist's room, all Diana would do was to blame herself and protect her abuser.

The therapist finally asked, what do you get from blaming yourself and protecting your abuser? What do you get out of protecting your abusive ex and blaming yourself instead?

This was a hard question for Diana, who finally said, I know I made him abuse me. I provoked him. There is something I could have done to make him treat me better. Earlier, he was very nice, and he used to make me feel confident. He always praised me and told me how special I was. I am not ready to accept that he had a personality disorder. There must be a way for me to get him back and fix things the way they were.

The therapist's view

It can be tough for Diana to heal from narcissist abuse. The reason is her history of being forced to believe that it is her mistake to be ill-treated. Her childhood was fractured; she was not appreciated. She fell quickly to the flattery of a narcissist partner. She is stuck and only wants to focus on the good part. We keep on wishing that she get back the excellent experience that first carried her away. Diana blames herself so much, thinking she would have done better if her alleged suitor had remained kind to her.

The reasons why a narcissist becomes abusive are to bring others down and keep them from outshining them. Furthermore, they do it to bring other people under their manipulations. They like being bossy. They feel fulfilled and secure when they know they can order people around them without resistance. A narcissist knows well that they cannot just control grown-up human beings as quickly, so they have well-mastered tactics to achieve it. The narcissist pretends, lies, baits, lures, destroys, and steals the sense of self from their targeted victims. They do their tricks in a much-hidden way such that the victims will not realize that they are succumbing to toxic manipulation.

Diana was taken through all the stages of therapy, and she is now reconciled with reality. The same Diana was told to write another statement of the real things that her mind tells her, but her brain does not want to believe.

What Diana wrote

It is not my fault that he was abusive. There is nothing I could have done to make him treat me better. He has a history of being offensive. He only treats women well in the beginning when he wants to seal the deal. He will eventually mistreat the other woman he is using to hurt me. Other men will find me attractive and love me sincerely .

The Fate of a Narcissist

It is very devastating to see a narcissist get away with their hurtful deeds. You have been traumatized, mistreated, abused, threatened, and deprived of your happiness, and then the narcissist abuser is basking in the sunshine, enjoying his new life to the fullest as if you had never existed. This makes you think that the order of things in the universe has no room for serving justice, even for a religious person, who finds their faith distorted and starts thinking there is no compassionate creator who watches over good people. In your mind, many unanswered questions can be tossed and turned; you are wondering why the wrong people get rewarded while the competent people get hurt and destroyed.

Let's try to answer some questions: Do narcissists enjoy the rest of their lives without karma serving them their just desert? Do they continue destroying people and getting away with it? The answer is no. No matter how long it takes, everyone ends up with what they deserve. This benevolent universe grants us divine compensation for what we have lost and immense tribulation to the abusers. We do not need to do anything to make this happen; it just happens naturally.

Getting the bigger picture of the fate of a narcissist can be the key to recovery. People often ask themselves, when is the narcissist going to pay for all the horrifying things they took me through? The truth is that they pay for it every second of their lives. You may not directly understand this, for maybe you see them succeeding in life with big cars, big houses, and new lovers who appears to outdo you while harbor your pain and loneliness, with no single penny to your name!

True happiness comes from within and not without. The most valuable riches one can possess are the riches of being your true self. This is one thing the narcissist lacks. Understanding this, you can start to connect, get passionate, and create wealth from other beings. Make sure what you do is heartfelt and sincere and whatever you attain brings peace and satisfaction. If only you release that distorted perception instilled in you by the narcissist, fulfilling success is on its way. This is opposed to the narcissist who doesn't experience their true self and has no permanent connections to anything. They may appear ambitious, for there are always fantasizing about new heights of success. But in reality, this is a perversion that costs them a lot. A narcissist does not find permanent happiness, whatever is exciting to them now will be lifeless and unworthy sooner or later.

Their need for a new supply of emotional and physical things is insatiable. Eventually, they get devastated. The universal system gives more than being to a person, and the narcissist ends up being more frustrated, and feeling more pain and emptiness than other people think. The narcissist is an accurate representation of a disconnect. They have a disconnect even with their cautiousness. They cannot experience love and any other life force. This makes it challenging to come out of their devastation. They further fall into drug abuse and other self-destruction activities.

Nevertheless, as a person who wants to heal and move on with life, it is good to focus not on where the narcissist will end up but on yourself. It is good to know that they will pay for their misdeeds. As for you, concentrate on yourself. Instead of stalking them to find out how much karma has done, focus your precocious energy on how to heal with life, get your true self back, and stand on your feet again.

A narcissist hides their true self. So, even if they are going through hell, they make people believe they are succeeding. If you base your happiness in seeing them suffer, you might not be pleased in the long run. Base your happiness on yourself, who you are, who you are becoming, and the good things that are on their way.

Narcissists' victims fight these dangerous narcissists who plan to ruin the lives of their innocent partners. You will successfully come out of stress and disappointments. The effect of many a narcissist has left several love partners ending their lives under messy conditions. Narcissists have significant effects on relationships and not to their benefit. the victims need to change their patterns with these narcissists' abusers. This can only be possible when they escape the narcissist's abuse. You will be able to distinguish yourself from people with this terrible disorder.

According to a variety of studies, narcissism happens mostly in men. The individual has a false sense of self-admiration while seeking excess respect from other people, both known and unknown to them. If not treated in a timely fashion, the condition can translate into more profound side effects. It escalates as far as affecting all people around the person. People affected by the disorder are not capable of tapping into other people's emotional world or showing any form of empathy.

A narcissist quickly flies off the handle at the slightest disagreement. They believe they are the "mighty superhuman" who is to be worshiped and never criticized. Propping up these delusions takes some work; hence, their dysfunctional attitude and behavior tend to stick around. They protect their imagination with defensiveness and rage at the slightest provocation.

Overall, these people are not capable of handling criticism and always disregard how other people feel. To date, this behavior remains a mystery, although a professional can diagnose the condition and treat it with therapy. Having knowledge of the number of people living with a narcissistic disorder offers some comprehension of the situation at hand. Knowledge improves outcomes for people living with this mental condition. The clinical life prevalence of narcissistic personality disorder is at 2-16%, and 1% for the general population. According to studies conducted by Twenge and Campbell 10 years ago, NPD has doubled. Studies also show that 1 in 16 people in the population are living with this condition.

Dealing with a narcissistic personally takes a toll on individuals, both psychologically and emotionally. First encounters with people who display this behavior see them as charmers until you start interacting with them. Be it at work, in a relationship, or as parents with children, you tend to feel some form of suffocation, or struggle with pain and loneliness.

In the end, narcissistic personality disorder has both physiological and physical effects. The physiological effects of NPD can have an immense impact on mental health. Some of them include zero interpersonal skills, hypersensitivity to criticism or insults, increased feelings of anxiety or depression, and low self-esteem. On the other hand, the physical effects of NPD come from various unhealthy behavior such as an arrogant attitude or behavior, over aggressiveness, the increased risk of abusing alcohol or drugs, and suicidal tendencies.

Since it is not a well-known mental disorder, people live with this condition despite the dire consequences. Seeking treatment is essential for the well-being of the person and their loved ones.

Conclusion

Narcissistic relationships are often complicated; many people who fall prey to narcissists never realize that they were involved in a relationship with a narcissist. There's a lot of information on the internet that explains how narcissism develops, but in order to understand it, it has to be experienced or observed firsthand.

Many of the signs mentioned in this book might not be visible from the outside but can lead to an unhealthy relationship if left unattended. It is also important that we become aware when someone we love is being abused because it can save their lives. Once again, dealing with a narcissist is not an easy task as they are great manipulators. They might start off as a soulmate and then reveal their true colors later on. While many narcissists will promise to love you forever, many will lead you on and leave you when they see an opportunity to get what they want somewhere else. Many people who are in relationships with narcissists tend to be idealistic and very naïve to the dangers of such relationships.

It is important to understand that love can be a very complicated concept, especially in the narcissistic world where everyone is very selfish. We are told from day one as an adult that we are our own person and we don't need anyone else's approval, but we should always strive for our own goals, ideals, ambitions, etc. However, when it comes to love, we might find it hard to understand the concept. Don't let your life become a complete waste by giving in to the narcissist's demands.

The Covert Narcissist

Recognizing the Most Dangerous and Subtle Form of Emotional Manipulation and Recovering from Abuse

Bianca Sutton

Introduction

Both narcissists and co-workers with an antisocial personality disorder (often incorrectly referred to as sociopaths) tend to be manipulative and lack empathy for others. They are both exploitative. While a sociopath represses empathy to avoid rejection, the covert narcissist represses it because he lacks self-esteem.

Narcissists are primarily concerned with their own needs and desires, while co-workers who have an antisocial personality disorder are mainly worried about others' needs. The covert narcissist has low self-esteem and fears that others will reject or humiliate him if he shows his true feelings. He is hiding himself to preserve his narcissistic façade of perfection despite his lack of an actual model of normalcy.

This condition is often apparent to others who are wise enough to understand what a narcissist truly is but tolerant enough not to confront the person about it. It is also evident to insiders, as they recognize the lack of essential regard for other people while avoiding confrontation for fear of negative consequences. Insiders may choose not to attempt to change the person, fearing he will become angry and violent towards them or dismiss his grandiose delusions entirely. Insiders might get hurt or lose their jobs in the process.

Covert narcissists often leave their co-workers and friends under the impression that they are well-liked and generally well-respected because of their strength of character, leadership abilities, and ease in making difficult decisions. However, in reality, they are very manipulative and controlling. They will often keep secrets from others about their true character and their need for validation. At their worst, they can even throw one person under the bus while throwing everyone else under too, except themselves, out of frustration and anger, leading him to become more violent towards even those he is closest to.

Chapter 1:
Origins of a Narcissist

D id you know that the term, narcissist, originates from Greek mythology? As the story goes, Narcissus, a very handsome man, disregarded the offers and advances of Echo, a nymph. As his punishment, he was cursed to love his image excessively in a pool of water. Gazing upon his reflection in the water for the first time, he felt utmost adoration, and he could no longer stop. Sadly, he was unable to enjoy nor consummate his love for himself. As Narcissus pined and yearned for a consumable love, he changed into a beautiful flower that bore his name, the narcissus.

The concept of self-adoration dates back to the early philosophers and psychologists in ancient history. In earlier Greek times, narcissism was thought to be hubris, defined as the state of extreme arrogance and haughtiness. Much later, philosophers in the 1900s further described it as being out of touch with reality when narcissism started to flourish in the budding school of thought known as psychoanalysis. Otto Rank, an Austrian psychoanalyst, was the first to publish a description of narcissism in 1911. In his studies, he connected narcissism with self-adoration and vanity.

Sigmund Freud furthered Rank's research in 1914 when he published a paper entitled, "Narcissism: An Introduction." Freud suggested that narcissism is associated with one's libido or the energy that drives a person to survive. According to Freud, an infant has innate selfishness because his libido is directed inward, a condition known as primary narcissism. Among babies, this condition is natural because they cannot do anything to acquire their needs but must rely on their primary caregivers or mothers. However, as the child comes of age, he starts to fend for himself. In turn, the libido shifts its direction outwards, relying on the adult's attachment of others. As a baby, he is used to being the center of attention – in the family's life. As he grows up, he realizes that this attention diminishes over time. This outward extension of the libido craves the affection of other people. It involves receiving love, care, admiration, and an appraisal from family and friends.

Sigmund Freud added that a child develops a self-image when he starts to interact with his environment. He begins to learn about social norms and cultural expectations. He conceptualizes an ideal image to pursue and attain. An essential key point from Freud's study is the idea that self-love and self-adoration may be transferred to other human beings or things. By giving away love, a person starts to diminish his primary narcissism, making him feel more vulnerable and leaving him less able to nurture and protect himself from several environmental factors. To replenish this security, Freud theorized that a person starts to feel secure and protected against all elements that aim to reduce his integrity by receiving love and affection.

It was not until the 1950s and 1960s that narcissism was classified as a disorder. During this time, Otto Kernberg and Heinz Kohut worked to shed more light on the concept. In 1967, Kernberg constructed the "narcissistic personality structure" and classified narcissism into three major types: normal adult narcissism, normal infantile narcissism (primary narcissism according to Freud), and pathological narcissism.

Finally, in 1968, Kohut understood more about the narcissistic personality disorder and took some of Sigmund Freud's ideas to support his theory. Narcissism then became a vital tool in "Self-Psychology," which suggests that narcissism is a normal part of early development. Kohut also theorized that a person's challenges and difficulties during his early "self-object" relationships affect his self-esteem later in life, leading to narcissistic disorders. It was not until 1980 that Narcissistic Personality Disorder (NPD) was born as an official diagnosis of this mental anomaly.

Narcissism is defined as having an excessive admiration of the self. Psychology describes the term as a deep sense of interest in the self-characterized by a lack of empathy. Narcissists are often characterized by high self-worth. This affects the thoughts and behaviors of an individual, as well as his interaction with others.

It is always easy to identify a narcissistic person in a group of people. Such individuals always excite the crowd and keep sharing stories about themselves. Narcissists tend to be manipulated and often lack a sense of compassion. Other traits associated with this personality include:

· I crave appreciation and acknowledgement, even when nothing has been accomplished.

· Appreciation of personal beauty and success.

· A feeling of being better than others.

· Exploitation and manipulation of others.

· Grandiosity and a high emphasis on self.

- Fantasies of being critical, famous or influential.

- Exaggeration of individual accomplishments and abilities.

1. Narcissistic Personality Disorder

Narcissistic personality disorder or NPD is a mental condition that makes people place more importance on themselves. The disorder is known to cause problematic relationship since patients often suffer from low self-esteem. It also causes issues at work, school and any other situation where collaboration is required.

Narcissists keep getting disappointed and unhappy when they are not given enough attention. Other people find it difficult to spend time around them because they always want to be pampered even when they do not deserve it.

Symptoms of the disorder include:

- High self-importance

This is one of the significant characteristics of NPD. It results in a high feeling of superiority, which often comes out as arrogance. Individuals with this disorder tend to believe that they are exceptional in some way and no one can understand them. They do not settle for average things since their standards are set too high. Therefore, they only associate with high-profile events, places and individuals. Because narcissists believe they are more important than others, they always demand to be recognized even when they have achieved nothing.

Narcissists are experts at fabricating lies and exaggerating situations just to get attention. They will never speak positively about others, even when an achievement results from a team effort. They make people feel indebted to them at all times.

· Fantasy

Narcissists are never absolute. They develop a world built on deception and imaginary thoughts. They create an atmosphere that glorifies them and does not consider themselves as failures. They love being in power and enjoy places where they are given total control. Such a world shields them from being ashamed about the reality of their lives.

Narcissists do not take criticism positively. Most ignore opinions and facts contrary to their beliefs. Any information or action that resists their fantasy is always treated with anger and defensiveness. Because they live in denial, it becomes difficult for others to create meaningful relationships with narcissistic people.

· Craving for admiration

To become good friends with a narcissist, you will need to praise him for every minor achievement - constantly. Individuals with this disorder survive on recognition and praise. That is why most of them surround themselves with individuals ready to shower them with glory and affirmation all the time.

· Feeling of entitlement

Due to their self-centeredness, individuals with narcissistic personality disorder keep expecting nothing but favors from others. They always get what they need. When associating with such a person, you must comply with their every demand. You are considered useless if you cannot do as instructed by the narcissist. If you do not comply, you will receive nothing except rage and ill-treatment in return.

· Exploitation

Narcissistic individuals can never connect with your feelings. It is almost impossible for them to identify with your pain or happiness. They can never put themselves in your shoes. Instead, they only manipulate you to get what they need. They see you as their servant, not the other way round. They will always take advantage of your availability to meet their needs. Narcissists never reflect on their behavior and how it can affect their relationship with others.

· Intimidation

If you are a person who fears getting intimidated, you cannot work with a narcissist. Narcissists can never get along with you if you seem to be more popular and talented. If you dare challenge any of them, you will be met with a high level of defensiveness. They will do everything just to make you appear inferior. If this does not work, they will end up insulting you or retreating from your presence altogether.

You need to understand that people with the narcissistic disorder can appear to be very charming. They always succeed in creating a very positive self-image. They come across as confident all the time and can easily lure you into believing in their fantasies. When dealing with them, you need to understand what they are looking for – admirers. Do not expect to receive any special treatment. You should treat a selfish person just as he is. To assist the person, you need to stop defending his lousy behavior.

· Setting helpful boundaries

Kindness and respect are some of the factors that characterize good relationships. One weakness narcissists struggle with is the inability to reciprocate kindness. They are unable to recognize others with importance because their needs always come first. To overcome this, they need to identify and set proper boundaries when dealing with other people. If you are a narcissist seeking to recover from the disorder, you need to highlight those things that violate your respect for others and deal with them accordingly.

· Learn to consider the feelings of others

Recovering from the NPD requires that you identify where the focus on self needs to end. It would help if you appreciated the existence of others by being aware of their feelings and thoughts. You can do this by:

· Speaking cautiously to others. When addressing them, call them by their names.

· Avoid talking too much. As much as you have a lot to share, it would be best to allow others to speak.

· Show interest in the affairs of others. Ask questions that make you appear concerned about the welfare of other people.

· Keep out of other people's space. Do not use their items or time without permission.

· Deliver substance

To reduce the anxiety and stress associated with the disorder, make sure that you deliver on your assignments. Doing this will eliminate the need to lie or exaggerate the results to gain appreciated. You will also get to enjoy healthier relationships built around friendship and trust. Some of the practical things you can do to achieve this include:

· Doing exactly what you promise. Keep your promises when it comes to appointments and agreements.

· Do not overpromise. It is better to under-promise and over-deliver.

· Take responsibility for any failures. Be accountable for the mistakes you make.

· Concentrate on impacting others differently. Do not engage in activities that will jeopardize your integrity. Also, avoid decisions that will make others feel manipulated and cheated.

2. Causes of Narcissism

Just as with many other disorders, the primary cause of narcissistic personality disorder remains unknown. However, it is believed that the condition arises due to specific childhood encounters, genetics, and psychological factors. Most people learn narcissistic traits from their seniors when growing up. Such features become difficult to stop and later develop into a disorder.

Some of the risk factors experienced in childhood that may trigger the disorder are:

· Having insensitive parents.

· Excessive pampering, praise and admiration with parents and other family members.

· Negligence when it comes to childhood care.

· Parents that over criticize their children.

· Childhood trauma and abuse.

· High-performance expectations from parents and family members

The disorder also occurs when the genes connecting behavior to the brain develop abnormally.

3. Narcissism and Society

Narcissism has existed for several decades. However, the concept has become rampant in the modern world as more cases are being reported every day.

Narcissists are masters at ignoring their limitations. Since they love themselves too much, they tend to live in illusion and self-deception to avoid facing reality. They do this by creating a false image of themselves clouded by numerous fantasies. Their true identity is hidden behind a mask that is not easy to identify. In reality, narcissists are suffering individuals who need a lot of assistance and understanding. As they continue to avoid reality, they develop a strong defense strategy that is difficult to overcome.

Although only a few narcissism cases get to the point a real disorder, almost every human being has at least one narcissistic tendency. It is a survival mechanism used to compensate for failures and shortcomings. People use it together with self-deception to avoid circumstances that lead to shame. It helps people overcome depression since most narcissists do not love themselves. Their narcissistic behavior helps them cover up their deep sense of inferiority and self-hatred.

Narcissists always project themselves as highly intelligent, eloquent and gifted. This projection comes out as arrogance and pride. They want the world to know how important they are. Their intention is never to hurt anyone, but their actions and feelings end up as emotional trauma for others. They feel no remorse for causing harm and may justify themselves to get out of awkward situations. Their main distinction is the lack of concern for their environment. They never bother about their actions and how they may affect their relationships. It is one way of getting attention from the world.

Narcissists are always indifferent towards the progress of others. They only get involved in activities that satisfy them. Their interest in other people's affairs is never genuine unless there is a platform for exercising their superiority. A good number of con artists in the world are selfish. Since they are deceptive, it is easy for them to con others and get away with it. Life becomes painful for them when they cannot achieve their selfish desires. They love it when people fear them.

A narcissistic person will change his personality or self-image based on the admiration he wants to receive from others. He will view himself through other people's eyes and then create a fake image that replaces what he sees. In reality, this image does not exist. A narcissist can assume a lifestyle that is not his just to remain in the limelight.

Narcissism is experienced everywhere. Narcissists can be your colleagues, family members or acquaintances. When it comes to the workplace, awareness must be created due to the arrogance and bullying nature of narcissism. By nature, selfishness remains a big challenge for organizations given the negative impact it causes on individual and team performance. Narcissistic workmates fail to realize the need for help. They will frustrate their colleagues and feel good when they get others into trouble.

When in the workplace, it is easy to identify a colleague with narcissistic traits. He or she will tend to:

· Inflate his ego and always force his way within the work environment.

· Never admit he is wrong even when a team has made a mistake.

· He will consider any mistake as someone else's fault.

· The narcissist will use mind control tactics to win other colleagues to his side. He may use the same technique to beat his boss.

Chapter 2:
The Covert Narcissist

Covert narcissists can be described as narcissists who don't fit into a narcissist's stereotypical personality profile. Covert narcissism may be more challenging to spot in several ways because of the narcissist's introverted character. Though it's just as dangerous as its extroverted counterpart, covert narcissism is a more hidden form of abuse and can be trickier to pinpoint.

The main thing a covert narcissist has in common with an extroverted one is that they both use superiority to cover their internal vulnerability. This, in turn, is also used to make their victim feel insecure or off-balance about themselves or the situation. While some narcissists might outright say, "I'm better than you, so play by my rules," a covert narcissist will instead strongly hint at it. They won't be direct about it, but you'll still feel the same degradation as if they'd said it directly.

While they may not display all the characteristics or behaviors outlined, a covert narcissist will demonstrate some of the following throughout their relationship with you. You may find that the covert narcissist in your life displays several of these traits or they only show them from time to time. Regardless, these ways of behaving should act as a warning, at the very least, and offer you the ability to spot when you've become the victim of a narcissist.

· Smugness

Being quietly observant, judgmental and showing gestures of superiority are characteristics you'll find in a covert narcissist. They tend to act with an air of smugness, which can leave you feeling belittled, confused, and often like you're simply not good enough.

When you're talking or taking "center stage" in a social setting, or even if it's just you and them, they will offer distant and uninterested behavior. However, when they're speaking, you may find that as well as the conversation being focusing on them and their views, they'll also attempt to belittle you and your opinions. Their critical, judgmental comments are, of course, very hurtful and humiliating.

· Highly Sensitive

Covert narcissists tend to handle criticism, or perceived criticism, very poorly. They deem negative feedback or constructive criticism as a personal attack on them. They react in one of two ways: they get highly defensive and use the smug superiority described above to dismiss any unwanted feedback, or they will sulkily withdraw from the situation.

Typically, a covert narcissist won't tell you outright what is bothering them, but instead they will let their cold behavior towards you let you know that something is up.

· Passive-Aggressiveness

Passive-aggressiveness in a covert narcissist can in becoming angry and hostile, and they'll often offer fake helpfulness with no intention of ever helping you. These passive-aggressive behaviors are expressed in covert ways, giving the narcissist an underhanded advantage over the situation. If an undercover narcissist feels threatened, they'll use passive-aggressive behavior to ensure they control the problem. These passive-aggressive tactics are a stealthy way to punish those who dare to hurt their fragile egos.

With a covert narcissist, this passive aggression will offer a thinly disguised sense of superiority, entitlement, and an unintentional way to showcase their arrogant view of the world. A covert narcissist is inclined to become hostile if they don't get their way. Even if their requests or demands are unreasonable, they'll devise stealthy yet destructive ways to make you miserable for hurting their delicate sense of entitlement.

Some examples of passive-aggressiveness include:

Verbal hostility: For a covert narcissist, putting other people down makes them feel self-assured and superior. This allows them to seek and obtain a false sense of importance, and their critical and hostile way of speaking to you will fuel their narcissistic fire.

In a nutshell, passive-aggressive verbal hostility from the narcissist is their habitual criticism of your ideas, experiences and feelings.

Hostile humor: Very thinly-veiled hostile banter or joking is often followed by the phrases, "I was just kidding" or "can't you take a joke?" Sarcastic, feisty humor offered by a covert narcissist is their way of expressing their internal anger, rejection or disapproval towards you.

Blaming: Blaming is a form of gaslighting for which narcissists are renowned. The intention behind the blameful behavior is to avoid any responsibility by manipulating the facts of the situation. A covert narcissist will distort your perception of a problem or conversation, therefore making it easier to place blame elsewhere. Often the undercover narcissist will misdirect the blame onto you, thus refocusing away from the real issue at hand: their failures and bad behavior.

Covert Sabotage: Covert sabotage is the narcissist's way of sneakily administering punishment on you in a very disguised way. Examples of this could be the narcissist deliberately disclosing hurtful and harmful information or deliberately obstructing positive endeavors or communications. Other examples could be the narcissist deliberately undermining any agreements you've made with them. The narcissist could also purposely overspend your agreed upon budget, this causing you financial difficulty - but of course, you'd be the person who gets handed the blame for this.

· Lack of Empathy

A distinct lack of empathy is a trait the covert narcissist shares with an extroverted narcissist. Both narcissist types are so self-absorbed and self-serving that they are dismissive of other people's feelings. Often, their apparent dismissiveness of your thoughts and feelings is, in fact, complete obliviousness to your senses.

Frustratingly, even when you tell the narcissist that their behavior or attitude is upsetting you or it'll result in dire consequences, their response will often be reverted back to them. Your needs, wants, thoughts, and feelings aren't the narcissist's main priority.

· the "I'm Special" Complex

A covert narcissist, although introverted, can still have a "special person" complex. They may heavily hint at being misunderstood, almost like they're so evolved that nobody can understand their genius or uniqueness. This "special person" complex is something the covert narcissist uses as a "woe is me" story: they may claim they feel isolated and misunderstood because they're so one-of-a-kind that nobody understands them.

Of course, this complex is just another way for the narcissist to bury his vulnerable and fearful true self.

· Impersonal Relationships

Covert narcissists are deeply insecure about their inability to connect with people in a meaningful way. They want to avoid being exposed for their interpersonal inadequacies and hide their incapability to forge deep relationships with others.

· Self-Absorbed

Self-centeredness and self-absorption are general characteristics of a covert narcissist. These introverted narcissists are destitute listeners and, as such, they form quick opinions on people and situations.

Quiet people are widely assumed to be good listeners, although this isn't the case; the opposite is true. Because of their self-absorption, they often find things that aren't about them (or things that will directly affect them) uninteresting and unworthy of their attention.

It's ironic that self-absorbed people, like the covert narcissist, also lack the self-awareness that the rest of us possess. While we are fortunate to have the ability to reflect on our actions and behavior, the narcissist is unable (or unwilling in a lot of cases) to fully recognize just how self-absorbed he is.

Most of us recognize the nuances of situations and understand that not everything always goes our way. However, covert narcissists generally only focus on their wants and, selfishly, what they deem to be agreeable. Anything else is uninteresting or a waste of time.

Hopefully, the above explanations have helped you understand what a covert narcissist is, and now you have some idea of the behaviors and characteristics that outline this type of narcissist. While this helps illuminate one type of abuse, pinpointing when you're the victim of a narcissist can be pretty hard to do, especially without guidance.

It's important to remember that the covert narcissist is possibly the most complicated type of abuse to spot. Generally, they look for highly empathetic people who will listen to their sob stories and give the narcissist the benefit of the doubt. Once the victim begins to feel a sense of responsibility for their narcissistic partner, and that's when the abuser knows they have them reeled in and they amp up their abuse in the relationship.

The victim is then trapped in a vicious cycle. Over time, the covert narcissist will make the victim question their perception of reality, doubt themselves, and accept blame readily. Because of this, the narcissist ensures that they won't be held accountable for their behavior by the victim.

As with all narcissists, covert narcissists do have a predictable behavior pattern for romantic partners. In the beginning, they may appear to idealize their partners. This acts as bait for their victims. Once the victim is hooked in, the narcissist will then devalue their partner, and (as you sadly may be all too aware), this causes the victim to chase the love and adoration they received from their abuser previously.

The victim is unaware that this devaluation from the abuser is done with sinister and purposeful intent. After this, the narcissist will then discard their partner.

The covert narcissist may appear as a calm, quiet and polite person to most people. However, when you're in a relationship with one, they're often cold, distant, abusive and demeaning. Jekyll and Hyde can be a good way of describing their personality and treatment of you.

Often, a covert narcissist is seemingly quiet and can usually be described as meek and inoffensive by most people, but behind closed doors, it can be a very different story. They thrive on their partners' failures and upset. It's not an uncommon game for a covert narcissist to set you up for loss or upset. The crazy-making thing about this is that the narcissist will then punish you for failure. Introverted narcissists are also renowned for making empty promises without ever having any intention of delivering. They will then get a twisted kick out of your reaction when they fail to provide, often making themselves appear as the victim and making you look unreasonable and selfish with unbearable expectations.

A hurtful and frustrating aspect to this behavior of making promises without delivering is when the narcissist will deny ever making that promise in the first place. This gaslighting behavior often makes you think you're losing your mind and makes you question your perception of reality. This is known as "perceptive*".

The best way to describe a covert narcissist's internal feeling would be "conflicted". While the narcissist wants to be worshipped and adored, and they think quite a lot of themselves, they are also incredibly insecure. This internal conflict creates the unbalanced, manipulative and willful confidence-sucker that is the covert narcissist.

Chapter 3:
Am I a Narcissist?

Narcissistic tendencies are always problematic, but there are times when it is worse than others. A "healthy" dose of narcissism can be beneficial. It is defined as having self-esteem while still maintaining a connection to others. It is self-love without being detrimental to others.

However, this isn't always the case. Sometimes narcissistic tendencies are extreme and need some profound changes. If this is something you fear might be affecting you or someone in your life, please read on for more information.

4. Sociopath

A sociopath is someone who is usually defined by a lack of empathy. Someone with an antisocial personality is often seen as a sociopath as they do not interact with others because people without this form of narcissism do. They're known for being very charming and likeable, but this is all a façade. Underneath all of that superficial falseness, they're calculating and have controlling behavior.

Here is a list of an indication to look out for:

· Being deceitful and lying. For example, they might con others and feel no remorse or use an alias to hide or what they're doing.

· An inability to follow social norms. They may act in inappropriate ways, from speaking out of turn to breaking the law.

· Overly assertive or aggressive behavior. It may be prone to getting into physical fights.

· An absence of empathy for others' feelings, even if they are responsible for those feelings.

· A display of very shallow feelings

· Impulsive behavior that hinders planning for the future.

· Lack of concern for others' safety.

· Irresponsibility that drives inconsistent behavior

· Taking part in reckless behavior, such as stealing, promiscuity, and taking uncalculated risks.

This behavior is worrying because it can lead to abusive relationships, aggression, and even violence. The longer people allow it to continue, the worse it will get. The further a sociopath will push the boundaries to see what they can get away with. It needs to be allocated right away to protect everyone who comes into contact with this person.

If you happen to identify with this list or know someone who shows no remorse for their actions, no matter what they've done, and they don't recognize that they need to change, then they might be a narcissistic sociopath. Studies have shown this often emanates from neglecting parents, sociopathic parents, or traumatic, abusive events. It can best be treated with a medical professional's help, and it's usually done via therapy.

5. **Psychopath**

Before this study, it has always been believed that psychopaths lack emotions and empathy, but it's more that they don't consider what will happen eventually. It all makes sense when the number of criminals who display these tendencies. Still, another research project found that fully functioning, successful adults with high-flying careers also show the same brain activity as a psychopath.

Here are some signs you can detect a psychopath:

· Superficial charm to lure people in at first

· Ignoring huge problems with a non-committal attitude

· An inflated sense of self

· A need for stimulation from extreme activities

· Lying, conning, manipulating

· Lack of guilt even when pain is caused.

· Shallow feelings, no depth of emotions

· No empathy

· Lacking control, promiscuous behavior, other behavioral issues

· Impulsive, irresponsible, no long-term goals

· A tendency towards criminal activity

The earlier these tendencies are spotted, the more chance you can help someone or even yourself. By letting these traits continue, you are letting it get worse. Psychopaths will use weaknesses against every victim to get what they want. The right thing to do is to extract yourself from the situation, if possible, before you get harmed. If this isn't possible, you need medical help for your loved one.

6. Narcopath

A narcopath is a narcissist-sociopath mix and is considered the worst type. Someone with an inflated sense of how important they are, as well as a constant need for praise and admiration – which already sounds exhausting! Relationships with them can be addictive but draining as the person with a narcopath will never win.

Here is an excellent checklist for identifying whether you are involved with a narcopath:

· Things move fast – really fast! Instead of getting to know you, a narcopath will immediately make you feel like you've found your soul mate.

· The compliments – at first, they might feel nice, but after a while, you might realize that they're generic and maybe a bit staged.

· Flattery comes in the form of comparisons. It is horrible if it links to an ex. Even if you come out on top, that won't last.

· You have strong chemistry. The passion is off the charts, but not much else is good.

· Hollow eyes that lead to nothing. It's all an act.

· The conversation constantly swivels back to themselves.

· A checkered relationship history is a sign of things to come.

· The silent treatment is standard.

It is another severe form of narcissism that can lead to abuse and violence if left untreated. Some therapy, primarily cognitive behavioral therapy, can help with this.

The red flags of manipulation include:

· Your words being used against you

· They offer you help, but their support leaves you confused and unhappy

· They say shocking things, then claim you misunderstood them

· A lot of what they do is designed to make you feel guilt and shame

· You question your sanity

· Love and affection are withdrawn once you don't obey them

· You fear losing that person, no matter what they do

· You always feel like you fall short of expectations

· You have been on eggshells with that person

· You feel isolated by them

If you feel any of these things happening in your life, you need to start thinking about taking some serious action. Read on for ways to help yourself and the narcissism sufferer.

It's seen as so beneficial that we even have some tips to help you gain some narcissism in your life to boost confidence when times are tough:

· Establish your own identity and don't worry about what others expect of you

· Feel proud when you reach your goals

· Give yourself affirmations

· Consider what you like about yourself

- Care for yourself
- Allow yourself to have imperfections
- When you feel bad, please do something to change it
- Share in the success of others

Chapter 4:
Falling in Love with a Narcissist

There are a lot of people who feel as if narcissists are drawn to them like magnets. It may not be that narcissists are more drawn to you, but you may be willing to hold onto them. When you see certain things, you may not recognize them as narcissistic traits, but they are still unfavorable. Since these are negative traits, most people will not go any further with the relationship.

People are often disturbed by the types of behaviors displayed by the narcissist. They will disengage from the situation because it is easier than dealing with someone problematic from the very beginning. The people who tend to stick around the narcissist will handle this type of situation in a very different way.

If you are a person who feels like narcissists are constantly drawn to you, take a look at your standards for relationships and what behaviors you will and will not tolerate.

To understand whether your standards are healthy and keep you protected, ask yourself the following questions.

- At any point in time, have you ended a relationship because of selfishness on your partner's behalf?
- Are you able to set clear boundaries and stick to them?
- Do you know what behaviors in a relationship you will tolerate and which ones are unacceptable?

- Do you rationalize staying in a bad relationship because you believe it can get better? Is this because of the way things started in your relationship?

- Do you allow your partners to devalue you?

- Is making excuses for your partner's bad behavior commonplace?

- Have you put up with mental, physical, or emotional abuse without leaving?

If you find that these questions relate to you, it is time to sit back and look over your standards. You need to find strategies to help weed out people with destructive behaviors before they sink their claws into you.

Exiting a relationship because you feel that someone is taking advantage of you or having a nefarious intent is not wrong. It may seem challenging to weed out the narcissists, but you simply give them more time to manipulate and take advantage of you when you give people too many chances.

There are also a few different personality traits that narcissists will pick up on and try to take advantage of. Specific characteristics are found to be more helpful to narcissists than others. If you are incredibly empathetic, have a desire to help others, are willing to try harder than most to make relationships work, or your sense of responsibility is strong, you are likely the perfect target for a narcissist.

All of these traits fall into the desires of a narcissist. They will do everything they can to take advantage of your kindness, compassion, and empathy. Most people don't try and hide the positive attributes they hold. Unfortunately, the narcissist can pick his target quite easily.

Narcissists also genuinely enjoy taking advantage of brilliant people. Everything in their lives is a game and roping, someone into their game who is smart feels like a significant win for the narcissist. The high they get from besting an intelligent person is better than many others.

7. Why are People so Attracted to Narcissists?

If it's true that narcissists are living in constant existential terror (whether consciously or not), why are people so attracted to them? Gradually, cracks begin to appear in the narcissist's idealization of you. He begins to realize that you are not a perfect being. This makes the narcissist feel insecure like maybe the floor could collapse. The narcissist feels betrayed by your failure to remain perfect. He may even become angry with you and start to criticize any tiny imperfection. The narcissist is projecting his insecurities onto you, filling you up with his bad feelings. You were once perfect, but now you are no good. The narcissist must distance himself. All the while, you are trying to understand what went wrong.

As this process unfolds, you start to become desperate to regain the good feelings you associate with being idealized. You become caught in the narcissist's gravity. The narcissist gazes longingly in the mirror, while you gaze longingly at the narcissist.

At the beginning of a romantic relationship with a narcissist, part of the scheme is that Mark will make Claire feel like she has found a regular Prince Charming. He will be everything for her and shower her with love and affection. He will give her everything she needs emotionally, and everything will seem perfect for a while.

This beginning "honeymoon" phase is essentially the hook designed to get Claire craving his constant affection. He will give her everything she wants sexually and be everything she needs in every other respect. Mark will be like a drug, and soon she will become addicted before realizing it. Even the most upstanding, strong, morally conscious, and intelligent people are still human beings with desires. Skilled narcissists will get under your skin and learn your deepest desires. Once this happens, you are at their mercy unless you pick up on the signs early and run as fast as you can!

Unfortunately, Claire does not see any signs of narcissism because she has never met a narcissist trying to manipulate her. She has never surrounded herself with people who were anything other than kind and compassionate, just like her. She loves that Mark has shown his vulnerable side, and he lets her feel like she is helping him through his pain, giving her a sense that she is offering as well as receiving. But over time, this will slowly fade away and reveal itself not to be the case any longer.

After a couple of months, perhaps, things will start to shift, as they always do. The timing will vary based on how the narcissist's plans are proceeding. But soon, the once hedonistic boyfriend is going to turn into something different, but at this point, Claire is madly in love with Mark, and what's worse, she trusts him. He starts to employ those emotional and psychological games which work to tear down her self-esteem and confidence gradually. He will introduce flaws and problems with her friends and family and incite arguments between Claire and those people in her life she loves and values. This will serve to slowly isolate her from those people she once trusted as she leans more and more on Mark, depending on what he tells her because he otherwise gives her what she needs, that is until he doesn't.

These emotional games will gradually tear Claire down until she is just a shadow of her former self. The narcissist may have already employed gaslighting techniques or now begins to introduce them as she focuses on the things that she now perceives are flaws in her character, body, or personality. Now and then, she will get a glimpse of the Mark she knew when they'd first met, and this will keep her going for some time. But it will gradually start to dawn on her that things are not what they seem.

One of the first things victims in his situation might pick up on is that the narcissist will become careless about consistency and repetitiveness because they do not care what others think or feel. When she confronts him about this behavior, he will easily deny it and tell her she is making things up—another gaslight symptom. It depends on the victim how far this will go.

Some people have strung along for years and years. Eventually, the narcissist will simply disappear and then reappear sporadically, telling his victim that he is unsure about things and feels insecure about their relationship, perhaps pointing out something that the victim has done wrong that makes him doubt her commitment, etc. The narcissist will use anything and everything at this point to inflict pain and make the victim feel like they need to make up for something they've done.

Eventually, the game is going to end, one way or another. Mark will have gotten bored with Claire and moved on. But frequently, the narcissist will not let go for a very long time, even if they are leaving for long periods between their reappearances. Depending on how strong their chains have become connected to their victims, these victims will simply wait, hope and pray until the next time they see their narcissist partners. The emotional pain and control have run so deep that they do not feel they can live any other way.

When we think of women in physically abusive relationships, many people find it too easy to simply pass judgment on the woman, suggesting that she just needs to leave. She just needs to go. The fact is until you've experienced the kind of emotional abuse and manipulation exercised by an abusive partner, it is impossible to understand just how much a person can twist another human being's reality.

Abuse victims often cite how they simply slipped into a state of denial or were so convinced they were the problem in the relationship that they merely tolerated the abuse and blamed themselves. It is a sad but true reality. Don't ever pass judgment on an abuse victim until you know what you're talking about. And even then, we must all realize that each of us is unique and we all have different constitutions, strengths, and weaknesses. How many times have you heard from someone that they never thought they'd be dumb enough to fall for that, etc.

It's important not to internalize a feeling of being "dumb" if you've fallen victim to narcissistic abuse. The fact is that these people do nothing with their lives except getting better and better at manipulating and hurting others. They are professionals, and they are experts. You are not an idiot for being human and having feelings. You have simply run into someone who knows exactly how to take advantage of your common human decency and kindness.

After the cycle of abuse ends and you've finally gotten free of the narcissist relationship, I hope that you can appreciate that you are lucky to have broken free at all. Many victims have strung along for the rest of their lives to die in misery and isolation without ever having received what they needed and wanted from a romantic partner. A victim going through emotional abuse knows that it is harrowing, and the effects are long-lasting. We now will talk about the emotional upheaval of ending a relationship with a narcissist and the impact of this experience in the long term.

Chapter 5:
Narcissistic Passive-Aggressiveness

When we think of passive-aggressive behavior, we often imagine a roommate leaving a sticky note on the bathroom mirror that pretends to be a friendly reminder to put the dishes away. The frustration they feel is thinly veiled. Passive-aggressive people are not aware of how openly aggressive their tactics are.

At some point, we have all been passive-aggressive. You might be trying to let out anger you know is fleeting. Maybe you think what you are doing will solve a problem while avoiding a confrontation. However, for some people, this is the way they navigate social interactions. They will not verbalize what they want. Instead, they leave it up to you to figure it out and then get upset when you don't. They do not dare to come to a person about something bothering them because they think that seems rude.

A passive-aggressive person is much more concerned about not appearing rude than they are about actually being polite. Not wanting to seem harsh is very different from genuinely being concerned about the feelings of others. Instead, their biggest priority is others' perceptions of them. That's why people-pleasing does not come from a selfless place. They will not stand in their truth. They do not know who they are, only that they want to be seen as a good person, and it is essential always to be considered the one in the right.

Emotional manipulators will do favors for you but do not be fooled. These favors come with strings attached. They will be used against you later. They will do things for people and give them gifts only to bring them up later when trying to get you to do something for them. The message will be, "Will you do me this favor? You know, because after all I've done for you, it's the least you could do?" You did not ask for anything. They gave these things to you out of their own free will. That is what makes these gifts nefarious. There was a secret plan, and now if you deny them their request, they say you are a taker and do not give.

The act of being passive-aggressive is a highly manipulative one, whether or not the person using it realizes this. Passive-aggressive people are masters at making it seem like they are leaving the choice up to you when they are secretly leading you towards a specific decision. For example, you are deciding where to go to eat. You suggest a restaurant, and they mumble a very unenthused "okay."

Their tone of voice makes it obvious that they do not want to go to that place at all. You ask them if there's somewhere else they want to go, and they say, "No, let's go there. It's where you want to go." It is highly manipulative because they imply that they will have to suffer through it if you pick the place. This manipulation forces you to let go of the idea, and in desperation for this to be over, you beg them to tell you where they want to eat. Then they say, "Can we go to that restaurant just this once? I usually go wherever you want, but I want to go there this time."

Passive-aggressive people will never say anything productive like, "I'd like to choose where we eat more often. Maybe we could take turns picking from now on?" It would mean that the pain is coming to an end. They expect you to be a mind-reader. You are supposed to know what they want even though they refuse to tell you, and then they get to be angry at you for not figuring it out.

Guilt trips are a favorite tactic among passive-aggressive people. Here is an example of a guilt trip. You have a group project, and on the day your group has agreed to work on it, your friend calls and tells you they have a problem. When you ask them if you can set up a time to talk about it later this evening, they respond with, "Oh, okay. I'll deal with this myself, even though I've listened to you when you needed someone. But it's okay, go work on your project. I know how important it is. I'll be just fine all by myself."

In this situation, even though you told them you would give them what they needed later, it does not keep them from pulling out the shaming tactics. In reality, it is they who won't give an inch, but through playing the victim, they have portrayed you as the unreasonable one who refuses to give anything.

Another of the most popular tactics for passive-aggressive people is the silent treatment. They will not tell you what they are upset about, but they will pointedly let you know that you have done something wrong. It is maddening because while they will not speak to you, they will not leave the room. It causes you to feel highly uncomfortable, which is precisely what they want. They will sometimes even get angry if you try to ask them what's wrong and tell you to leave them alone, but if you do that, you are "walking away" and not fighting for the relationship. You are in a no-win scenario. When they finally tell you all of their gripe, it comes out in a rush. It feels like a tidal wave barreling right at you.

A covert narcissist will often tell you nasty things while expressing emotions of sadness. For example, they will tell you they cannot forgive you for something while at the same time crying. This way, you don't get to be angry at them for what they say to you.

Covert narcissists claim not to be able to express their anger. Ironically, they spend most of their lives angry. Their rage is silent, and it builds up over time. They become bored with the relationship they are currently in, so they start talking to someone else, telling them that all of their partner's shortcomings while conveniently forgetting to mention what they have done wrong. They say this to get sympathy for having put up with such mistreatment.

The cheating has already begun when this happens because they are no longer working with their partner. They spend long hours with another person, speaking badly of their partner, building themselves up as a martyr, while the person they are talking to is saying things like "I'd never do that to you."

Both the narcissist's partner and the person they are speaking ill of are being manipulated because the person outside the relationship is being led to believe they would never be spoken of like this. This is because they are not being given the entire story. They are being told a mere fraction of the truth. The narcissist leads them to believe their partner is the source of all of the relationship problems.

That's why it is so important to be cautious of a person who has nothing good to say about their partner and is talking to you about all the problems in the relationship. It means when they have a conflict with someone, they put all of the blame on the other person and will not take any for themselves. If you are thinking about entering into a relationship with someone like this, there are a few things you need to consider first.

First and foremost, this person makes you feel like there is a chance for the two of you to get together while you are already in a relationship. This means that loyalty is not their strongest suit. They might have you convinced that their partner is the source of all of the relationship problems, but that is one extremely biased account. You have not heard the partner's side of things. If they turn to somewhere outside of their current relationship, they will do the same when the two of you have a problem. Right now, you are bright and shiny because they are love-bombing you and because you haven't spent any real time with them. but make no mistake, you will fall from grace. The question is not if it will happen, but when.

Right now, their partner is the problem. All of their anger and hatred is currently directed at them while you are the one bright spot in their life. You are in the honeymoon phase. If you get into a relationship, their partner will no longer be around to be a scapegoat for their misery. This means that the job will be relocated to you. A narcissist must have someone to place the blame on for their unhappiness. They will not recognize their role in it if they are not satisfied with their life. Something is missing within themselves, but they assume it is because of something the people in their life, especially their romantic partner, are failing to provide for them.

Think about a child who constantly wants a new toy. They have an entire collection of toys that they have not played with for months, and they are poorly taken care of. They think the source of their unhappiness is that they do not have the latest stuffed animal they have their eyes on. They feel like something is missing that will be satiated once they get that particular toy. They genuinely believe they will somehow treat this toy better than the others once they have it because it is unique.

This behavior is expected out of a child, but over time they should learn to value their things better than that. Better loyalty should be instilled into them. Narcissist never grow out of this juvenile way of thinking. The only thing they grow out of is playing with toys. When they get older, they will apply that same mentality to friendships and relationships. The person they are currently dating will no longer be exciting, and they will want someone new.

Chapter 6:
Living with a Narcissist? Do and Don'ts you Should Know About

Working with a narcissist or interacting with one during social gatherings is one thing, but if you live with a narcissist, several instances could lead to friction. Research says that living with a narcissist can lead to toxic relationships; that is true if the narcissist is suffering from very high degrees of NPD and is beyond all help. However, if you are careful about some of the things you do or do not do while living with a narcissist, you can avoid much of the relationship's friction.

8. The Dos and Don'ts of Living with a Narcissist

• Praise the narcissist from time to time: Narcissists thrive on appreciation. The one thing that keeps them going is praise and approval from others. Humor your narcissist partner from time to time and praise him. This is also true for a woman. This might seem at first that you are only enabling the narcissist behavior, but actually, you are not. Praising him will make him feel you notice him, and chances are that a covert narcissist will also attempt to notify you, even if the circumstances are slim. Yet, it is better than nothing and can establish a relationship of quid pro quo.

• Set clear boundaries: We have spoken about this before. As soon as you start living with a narcissist, be clear about your requirements. Tell him that he can have anything around the house as he wants it to be, as long as you get to have some things as well. The same goes for other areas of your life. Sticking to these parameters and setting boundaries from the very beginning provides a foundation for a stable pattern later.

• Expect them to push back: As soon as you set your boundaries or become assertive, expect them to move around and encroach on your personal space. Narcissists have a hard time dealing with the fact that you have a life of your own or one that does not involve them. So they will put up significant resistance to ensure that you do not always get the things you want or will most likely throw tantrums like a child to get your attention. Stick to your guns, and once they see how strong you are, they will be forced to adjust to your point of view, even if only a little.

• Find a support system: A support group should comprise people you would stand with you through thick and thin. They could be your parents, your best friend, or a colleague at work. If you do not have anyone because you are far from your people, you can always join a therapy or counseling group. The point is to have an outlet where you get a chance to speak for yourself and vent your frustrations without being judged. The narcissist partner at home will have little time or regard for what you have to say, so make sure others are around you.

• Insist on concrete results: When you start living with a narcissist, you will find many occasions when the narcissist promises you this and that, but then you'll notice they never come through. This is one of the many aspects of narcissism; manipulating people and making empty promises to convince the other person to get what they want is a pervasive trait. Put a stop to this as soon as possible and insist on immediate action.

- Expect other kinds of disturbances: A person with NPD is prone to different types of problems. They could be into substance abuse, or there could be similar problems. A narcissist will need professional help and therapy at some point in time, and that is beyond your power.

- Be open about receiving help yourself: Not just your partner, but you should also be mindful and open to the idea of receiving professional service when the time comes. Do not hide your frustrations under the garb of "I am fine" because you are not. The more you acknowledge your predicament, the better you will be able to deal with it.

- No matter what, it only makes sense to focus on the bright side from time to time to make coping easier. A covert narcissist is not always a wrong person; there might be other traits in him that are genuinely good, and he might be good at other things. Focus on them and see how it can enhance both your lives so that co-habiting becomes easier.

- When you decide to live with a narcissist, it is mainly because you might have seen some good in him or he or she has attracted you in some ways. When you do confront the more complex and dark side of a narcissist's personality, it might come as a rude shock to you but do not be in a state of denial about it. Do not try to overlook his possessiveness seeing it as genuine care or his controlling nature as looking out for you.

- Do not internalize what the narcissist says. A narcissist will chastise you in front of others, and they may make remarks about how you are nothing without them at your side. This is designed to make you feel bad about yourself and learn more about the narcissist, which is just what the narcissist wants to satisfy his ego.

- When you live with a narcissist, they automatically assume that you are there because of him, and you should devote your time to him alone. While giving him some attention from time to time is essential, do not make yourself too available. Do not be at his beck and call. Even if you are in the house and the narcissist wants you to do something, tell him you are busy with something else and you will get it done in due time. Chances are, whatever he was asking you to do was for his satisfaction. Do not make it a habit to become the source of his gratification every single time. Distancing yourself from time to time from the very beginning will prevent the formation of a toxic pattern later.

- Do not give in easily: Resist the narcissist from time to time and do not always give in easily to whatever he says. It might seem tempting because giving in to the narcissist's wishes is the easiest way to avoid friction. However, if you make that a pattern, you will be in danger of losing all sense of self. You have to understand that if you make it a habit to give in to whatever he asks, you will completely deprive yourself of everything that is rightfully yours.

- Do not lose yourself: Do not lose yourself when you are in a relationship with a narcissist. Living with a narcissist involves giving him a lot of attention. Do that from time to time because that is what he needs, but do not lose yourself in the process. Take those opportunities to get to shine yourself; dress up every once in a while and revel in the praises people shower on you.

- Do not try to put the narcissist in their place: This can be very tempting, and it is also the only natural to give them a taste of their own medicine from time to time. However, expect a severe backlash from the narcissist when you do that. They are not used to rejection and cannot stand being reprimanded for anything - because they can do no wrong. Trying to put them in their place could lead to volatile situations, so do not engage them aggressively. Being firm but also patient is the best approach with narcissists.

• Do not expect empathy: The sooner you come to terms with this, the better for you. Narcissists are not capable of empathy. A covert narcissist will try because they are usually less aggressive than their overt counterpart, but empathy is something that people with NPD are not capable of. Hence, they will not feel bad for you. Some might articulate that they do, but it is not going to be heartfelt. You need to judge for yourself how much of this you can take and for how long. Make sure you have people around you who will empathize with you in the difficult times when the narcissist does not.

• Do not be afraid to think of alternatives: It is alright if you feel that you want to stay with your partner even if he is a narcissist. However, give considerable thought to your alternatives should you choose to leave. Please do not start thinking that your lives are inextricably linked, and never let yourself believe that you are nothing without him.

Research shows that narcissists are incapable of forming bonds, so they hardly have long-term relationships. Sooner or later, their partners tend to leave, and you could be one of them.

The alternatives could be anything: you could move to a new neighborhood or a new city if you happen to get a new job. You could go back to the things you loved the most but never had the time to indulge in because almost all your time was devoted to your narcissist partner. You could think of dating again when you are ready and accept that not everyone is a narcissist.

Chapter 7:
The Language of Narcissists

The narcissist can seem unfathomable to the uninitiated. They are adept at manipulation, both emotional and otherwise such that most of their targets do not realize they are being manipulated. Indeed, the narcissist can be construed as an animal a little different from the rest of us. From their motivation to control how they are they perceived or see themselves, they are wired a little differently.

We can thus speak the language of narcissists. When one understands what motivates the narcissist and how they perceive others, one can understand how to protect themselves against them and begin the healing process. Not all narcissists are the same, so understanding narcissists' language starts with learning about the different types.

Men and women with narcissistic personality disorder all have the same essential characteristics - vanity, superiority, entitlement, a lack of empathy, bullying and belittling, and others - but how they manifest can differ. Indeed, the reader will discover that although all narcissists can manipulate and be abusive, others can be worse. This goes without saying. The narcissist may be the type who can engages in a long-term relationship, even if that relationship is fraught with misery for their partner. Or the narcissist can be the type that is so destructive and vindictive that they create a path of destruction all around them in a relatively short period.

9. **Types of Narcissists**

The narcissist partner may readily appreciate the traits that help make the diagnosis of the personality disorder. Still, by exploring further the manifestations of this condition, a more robust defense against them can be maintained.

There are many different ways of categorizing narcissism. The primary division in narcissism is between those whose vanity and superiority stem from external characteristics versus those who have grandiosity based on something internal. But as we will see, narcissism can also be categorized based on other factors. It is even possible for a narcissist to have features from more than one type of narcissist.

The narcissist is a strange bird, though the person may not know it. Their vanity and superiority seem natural, and it is normal and natural for them to act based on these characteristics. This is true of all of the different types of narcissism. The following is a list of the major types:

· Somatic narcissism

· Cerebral Narcissism

· Overt Narcissism

· Covert Narcissism

· Seductive Narcissism

· Vindictive Narcissism

· Somatic Narcissism

We tend to think of narcissists as vain based on their appearance, but this is not true of all of them. Indeed, shoving the narcissist into this superficial box allows most to go unnoticed, poising them to wreak havoc on their loved ones and the others around them. The narcissist can have delusions and a sense of superiority based on an external factor, or they can be vain about something that others cannot see, like their intelligence.

The somatic narcissist is the type that is overly concerned with their appearance and sees this as a source of superiority over others. It does not have to be the case that the narcissist actually is better-looking or more fortunate somehow than others; they only have to perceive that they are. It is easy to stereotype everyone who is vain about their appearance as a narcissist. Still, the somatic narcissist engages in the other behaviors and has different thought processes associated with this personality disorder, such as entitlement, and being belittling and demeaning, a need for admiration from others, envy, and lack of empathy.

10. Cerebral Narcissism

The cerebral narcissist can easily fall under the radar. We do not often think of narcissists as vain or superior about their intelligence, sense of humor, personality, or other qualities about themselves. Still, the cerebral narcissist sees these qualities as the repository of their inflated self. The cerebral narcissist can be a stealthy manipulator and abuser because they do not fit the bill of what most people think a manipulator or abuser looks like.

The cerebral narcissist may not be particularly attractive or prepossessing. We think of the narcissist as obsessed with their appearance—like Narcissus staring at his reflection in the pool—but this type can seem relatively unconcerned with the externals. But they are still narcissists. This type of person may belittle and abuse others based on their perception of a lack of intelligence in the other person. They may be superior in their charm, sense of humor, and great personality. These individuals can be hazardous because they may have internal qualities that attract others to them. These people are just as entitled, envious, and lacking in empathy as the somatic narcissist, charming or not.

11. Overt Narcissism

Narcissism can be characterized by how explicit the actor is in expressing their qualities to others. Indeed, we can think of narcissistic traits as being those that are more obvious, like bullying and belittling, and those that are more covert, like envy and a need for admiration. The covert narcissist is the bully who is not reticent to demonstrate to others how little they think of them. These are not the seductive charmers who fool everyone; these are the people who place themselves on a pedestal from which they look down upon others - a pedestal that everyone can see.

12. Covert Narcissism

All narcissists can hide their true selves in order to slither their way into the good graces of others. As a discussion of overt narcissists suggests, if narcissists are honest about who they are, most people would dislike them and be immune to their manipulation. The most effective manipulator and the abuser are the ones who wear an attractive mask, whether it is an external or an internal one. A good manipulator can get you to like and trust them. This is the covert narcissist, the person who acts in secret, perhaps hiding their true nature even from themselves.

13. Seductive Narcissism

The seductive narcissist does not have to use their body or appearance to gain influence over others. Indeed, the seductive narcissist can be a cerebral narcissist who charms with their winning conversation or great sense of humor. Hot narcissism refers to men and women who wheedle themselves into the confidences of others. This does not have to be a beautiful woman in four-inch heels or a young man with 20-inch biceps and a six-pack. This can be the comedian or the life of the party who is just as effective at seducing women as the men who are more favored phenotypically (if not more so).

14. Vindictive Narcissism

There is a reason why narcissism is included in the dark triad of perilous disorders. The narcissist is vain and entitled, but he also tend to tear down and destroy them. Some narcissists are more adept at this type of behavior than others. The vindictive narcissist represents the most dangerous subtype of this disorder. We think of vindictive behavior resulting from a slight that sets the other person off. Still, the vengeful narcissist can be triggered by something so minor that it is barely noticeable.

The vindictive narcissist may be inspired to destroy you because you did not attend their birthday party, or you went but were better dressed. Perhaps they noticed their boyfriend spending a little too much time looking at you. The vindictive narcissist desires to destroy you because they are envious of your intelligence, or maybe they just do not like you. What matters is that the vindictive narcissist operates with solid weapons. They will use their words to turn everyone around you against you, even suggesting to others that they should harm you in some way. Vindictive narcissism is more common than people think, and these individuals share a comfortable cell in evil with the Machiavellian and the psychopath.

15. Manipulation Psychology Used on the Mind of the Victim

We have spoken much about manipulation as the art of the narcissist. We have not delved more deeply into the psychology that the narcissist uses to exert their influence. Narcissists understand human behavior very well, and they know just how to establish power over others. Manipulation psychology is not just about using words to get the target to do this or that; this type of mind control also involves using gestures and being conscious of others' gestures to engage in a kind of suggestive play that most targets are oblivious to.

16. Recognizing This Type of Mind Control

This type of manipulation is most effective in the beginning of a relationship. Although the narcissist may still have some learning to do as far as reading you is concerned, they will use their manipulation psychology tactics to gain power over you at this stage. The narcissist knows that human beings like to establish rapport with others. Members of our species naturally engage in this sort of dance, so they will use their tricks to develop a rapid and unnatural connection. They will note your subtle gestures, like hand or head movements, and they will copy them.

Though this may seem a silly thing to do, this is a type of suggestion or mind control that causes the other to identify subconsciously with the person copying them. Even ordering the same thing at a restaurant or liking the same things you want, like television shows or movies, is a way of establishing rapport through manipulation. This allows the narcissist to engage in mind control because once they have proved this rapport, you are more vulnerable to suggestion.

It is essential to recognize this type of mind control to break free from the narcissist's hold. Most likely, you have not realized how much information you have given the narcissist. They know your moods and gestures and how to copy them when necessary. And you can easily recognize this type of mind control when you are doing things not in your best interest or when the words of the narcissist make you feel a particular way or seem incongruent with their facial expression (which may be seductive).

Chapter 8:
Narcissist Abuse

According to the Diagnosis Statistics of the NPD, between 0.5% and 1% of the overall population have the disorder, and 50% to 75% are said to men. Mostly narcissism is practiced in learning institutions. Narcissism can be between child-child, adult-adult, or child-adult. Narcissists portray puffed up and irrational traits. These are the same traits used to abuse others. Below are their signs and how they use them against their victims.

Magical thinking: Narcissists use distortion and hallucination known as magical thinking to see themselves as superior and perfect to others.

Entitlement: A narcissist always expects a lot of favorable treatment because they consider themselves unique. Failure to do so they underrates their superiority. They will call you a difficult or awkward person if you fail to comply with them.

Bad boundaries: Narcissists believe that other people exist to meet their needs. There's no boundary between them and others.

Arrogance: A narcissist who feels deflated tries to regain their sense of self-adoration by humiliating, diminishing, and embarrassing someone else.

Shamelessness: They are proud and act shamelessly and never mind about the emotions or wishes of others.

Envy: They envy other people's abilities and may use contempt to depreciate them or their achievements.

Exploitation: Narcissists involve themselves in exploiting others without minding their emotions or interests.

17. Who is Affected By OCD?

Narcissistic abuse can end in ignoring the behavior, forming relationship triangles, physical abuse, belittling comments, contempt, and sabotage. When there's a fight or an argument between a narcissist and an opposing party, narcissists tend to change the story and present only the parts where the malicious party/person reacted to their narcissism. They later frame it as if that's where the misunderstanding got started.

If they dislike you and intend to bully you, but you happen to defend yourself, they will truncate the story and frame it as you're the bully. They like to spread false information about the person they dislike by gossiping, slandering, and smearing them.

18. The Sadistic Words of a Narcissist

Narcissists use words to lure their targeted victims. They master very well when, where, and how to strike with their verbal tricks. They have the forked tongue of both sugar and venom. When the ideal time for full brown abuse comes, they become very generous in throwing poisonous and rotten verbal apples, well-tailored to confuse, belittle, and degrade their prey. Their well-calculated mind games are meant to damage those on the receiving end. They devalue their victims to make them lose their self-worth worth so they can submerge them into their selfish will. Victims are left traumatized, with a great deal of emotional pain.

The pain caused seems to be unending; they can become mentally disabled.

19. Low-Level Abuse

These consist of small, weird comments. In the beginning, they may seem insignificant, but they form the foundation of a narcissist's verbal abuse. This is how they begin to take control of their victims. This often starts early in the relationship. A friendly smile accompanies seemingly insignificant comments; hence, they are rarely recognized for what they are. The victim merely knows that this hidden abuse will advance and continue throughout the relationship.

20. The Special Union Myth

This is also done mainly at the beginning of a relationship. It is done to convince the victim that they have a special and unique type of companionship.

They may use phrases such as "I have never met a special person like you before." This forms the platform for the victims to feel obliged to tolerate future harmful abuse. They are groomed into thinking that what is between them and the narcissist is exceptional and beyond the ordinary.

The victims are conned into buying into the deceptive idea that the best relationships are explosive and passionate. In these delusions, they never see the signs of abuse trickling in. Even when things fall into a dead-end, they encourage themselves to remain the unique element in their union. With every passing day, they find it very difficult to break things off.

21. The "I Didn't Mean It" Tease

At this point, the narcissist constantly dismisses insults or criticisms, claiming that they didn't mean what they said. They know very well that the initial comment wounds their prey but makes up excuses to conceal their malicious intention. In reality, this is their way of tactically going on the offensive to put themselves permanently into a dominant position.

22. False Compliments

Charming and complimentary phrases are the essence of another skill that most narcissists have mastered well. They can praise other people when it suits them, but not a single word is heartfelt. The false praise is to manipulate others, get them onside, and make the criticisms that follow go unnoticed. They may say things like, "I like your character; you are cool and understanding." In other words, this is a means of softening the blows that will follow.

These compliments may seem harmless to the victim and any onlookers. In a way, they may even seem honest. On the contrary, they are just a package of sugar-coated lies. The narcissists themselves don't believe in what they are saying, but it serves their purpose well. It is meant to bait their target.

23. Projection

A narcissist is never ready to come to terms with reality. Acknowledging their fails, dysfunctional behavior, and malicious intentions are something they are never willing to do. Anything short of perfection is not something they wish to see in themselves. To achieve this, all their faults are projected onto their victim to shift the blame.

24. Tone Changing

Narcissists can manipulate language with different techniques to get their way. Narcissists employ the most powerful use of language to pursue a silent approach and reach the end goal of the course. During a confrontation, they may choose to glare, frown, shake their heads, turn away, speak softly, or raise their voices. They alter the volume of their voices to convey different messages.

A narcissist applies whatever approach to language is appropriate in their mind. Their words are packaged with venom to poison and bring down the other person. Their intentions are evident to them, but they may demonstrate a different perspective to others. All this is carefully calculated to lure the victim to fall under their control.

25. How Narcissist Traits can be Harmful

The word "narcissism" is sometimes taken lightly. A better understanding of the term is important. There are some less harmful traits of a narcissist, but these do not matter much. But some of their extreme misdeeds can be toxic to other, and this one matters a lot. These toxic traits are the ones they use to lure, manipulate, and abuse their victims. Let's unpack these harmful behaviors.

1. An exaggerated sense of self-importance

We realize that arrogant people when they need to overstate themselves try to cover up their fragility. The irony is that their need to be recognized as superior has no tangible achievements to back it up. They do nothing to deserve the kind of respect they demand. They look down on others to feel more important. This kind of behavior can be harmful to the people around them.

2. Preoccupation with fantasies

They are preoccupied with always thinking about themselves. The narcissist has an altitude that it is all about them, and others only matter as much as they are helping them achieve their selfish needs. They live in a distorted world where they fantasize about being the undisputed hero. They believe they are above everyone. If you try to outshine them, they will take you down, notch by notch, until you are under their feet. This can mean being harmful to those they strive to take down.

3. Special and unique

In their fantasies, the narcissist believes he is of a higher class. They see themselves as too big to fit into the ordinary slots. They think they can only associate with people on the top of the ladder of success. People with narcissism believe that other people should be regarded according to what they do and not what they are. They do not assign value to the connections they have with their friends. They do not consider values and personal characteristics.

4. An insatiable need for admiration

For a narcissist, the need for admiration can never find satisfaction. They are empty emotional vessels with a hole at the bottom. You eventually run dry and mercilessly yearning for more.

5. Extreme sense of entitlement

Narcissists think highly of themselves, and they expect other people to treat them the same. They believe their expectations should be met without hindrance. The entitlement of the narcissist is hard to live with because it leaves out anyone else's needs. The narcissist's needs always come first. They feel they deserve the royal treatment, and if you are compliant, they will take you down, make nasty comments about you, try to hurt you, and withhold your rights. This is a relationship that can lead to severe depression.

6. Being exploitive

Narcissists take advantage of others to achieve their ends. The narcissist is never afraid of taking advantage of others to satisfy their intentions.

7. Lack of empathy for others

The narcissist is always unwilling to pretend to identify with the feelings and needs of others. They will do a false show of compassion, but it is impossible to sustain because it is just meant to achieve their purpose. As soon as the other party seems not to be cooperating, the true self of narcissist blossoms. Narcissists are not able to tune into other people's feelings. They direct every conversation back to themselves. They ruthlessly turn against the other party.

8. Envious of others and anticipating that others are envious of them

Since narcissists live in an imaginary world where they are undisputed heroes, they believe they are highly admired. They imagine that other people are jealous of their entitlements. They claim that others are envious of them. Their ego gets threatened by anyone who has the potential to outshine them. In the projection of their envy onto others, they do nasty things to bring down their anticipated competitors.

9. Arrogant behaviors

This is a cover-up for their fragility and low self-esteem. It looks like narcissists have a high self-love, but in a real sense, they may be self-loathing. They take others down to feel better about themselves. They make others pay the price of their feeling of vulnerability, self-pity, and anxiety.

This trait is typica of people who have no apologies. Their arrogant nature makes them never acknowledge that they are be wrong. Even when they know very well that they are the one who messed up, they try their best to ensure that someone else carries the blame.

Chapter 9:
Gaslighting

Gaslighting refers to a type of psychological abuse used by narcissists to infuse in their victims an extreme sense of confusion and anxiety to the extent that they no longer trust their perceptions, memory, and judgments.

Gaslighting techniques used by narcissists are similar to those used in interrogation, torture, and brainwashing. These techniques have been predominately used in psychological warfare by law enforcement agents, intelligence operatives and covert agencies for decades. It is intended to systematically target the victim's mental stability, self-esteem, and self-confidence to disallow them from functioning independently.

When a victim is being gaslighted, the abuser systematically withholds factual information and replaces it with false and misleading information.

Gaslighting is a subtle manipulative tactic. Thus, it is difficult to detect, and with time, it completely undermines the victim's psychological stability. It is a hazardous form of abuse because it results in significant damages (victims lose the sense of themselves). When they've been gaslighted over some time, they lose trust in their judgments and even degenerate to the point of questioning the very essence of life. They not only don't second guess themselves, but they also become highly insecure when it comes to decision making.

Furthermore, these victims fall into depression and become withdrawn, making them dependent on their abuser for their sense of purpose and reality. Gaslighting takes away the victim's identity and purpose and replaces it with self-doubt and emptiness.

26. Gaslighting in Relationships

The people that use gaslighting the most are abusive partners in relationships. A narcissist in an abusive relationship will try to convince the whole world that it is love and intimacy, but the truth is, it's nothing but manipulation. Gaslighting in itself negates genuine love and affection.

Narcissistic relationships follow a pattern, and when it gets to the stage where the abuser begins to show his true colors, he will start to dish out his gaslighting techniques. For example, let's say you and he had plans to go out over the weekend, but when you called to remind him a few days later, he backtracked, saying something like, "I can't remember having such discussion with you, are you sure I'm the one?"

It looks like an innocent response, and at this stage, you won't read too much meaning into it because you're still in a state of bewilderment. Perhaps it might look like you remembered wrong or misheard. When something like this happens in isolation, it might not be gaslighting; it could be that you genuinely forgot, or there was a mix up somewhere. However, when it becomes a consistent occurrence, then questions need to be asked.

As time goes on, you'll start to notice more inconsistencies between the things the narcissist abuser say at different times. For example, you may suggest the idea of visiting a spa for a massage because in the past, he loved going to the hotel. But this time, he might say something like, "I hate going to the spa. Let's go to the beach instead."

Now, it gets a little bit confusing, and you begin to doubt yourself. Was it someone else who said they like spas? Or has the story changed? Suppose you're convinced that they made the earlier statement and are now saying something else. In that case, this might be their way of suppressing and manipulating you into believing that you're not attentive enough.

When the gaslighting moves up to the next level, the abuser will now begin to insinuate that you are the one who is now backtracking from your earlier assertions. How the narcissistic abuser presents the matter depends on the stage of the relationship, but this is an example of such conversation:

Victim: I just informed my mom and dad that you're attending our Christmas dinner. They can't wait to see you.

Abuser: Hey, but we agreed that we need to take some time before we involve family, didn't we?

Victim: But we had this discussion some days ago, and you said you were more than happy to attend

Abuser: I would love to meet your parents, but I told you that we should give it some time. You even agreed. However, the deed is done, and I won't disappoint your parents, so I'll attend.

If you study the conversation above, you'll realize that by agreeing to attend, the abuser is acting friendly and accommodating. As the gaslighting progress, the abuser will continue to explore new methods. From dishing out lies as a response to your statements and questions, they'll begin conversations with lies concerning things done in the past. For example, they'll say something like," You told me I could borrow your credit card, right? Well, I have just bought some items online. I'll make a refund next week.

This time, they cooked up a conversation that shows that you permitted them to spend your money. However, you're convinced that you never did, and they know you didn't, but if you decide to talk about it, they'll concoct more lies and ultimately cloud your mind with some believable stories. Again, this is just a way of increasing your self-doubt in order for them to assume control over your possessions, feelings, and life.

Finally, when the abuser starts to notice that your resolve is getting weaker and weaker, they'll substitute covert deception for straightforward lies. Thus, they will lie about things they/you did or didn't do and things they/you said or didn't say. For example, let's say you started heating water for coffee and had to leave to take care of something else. But when you returned, you saw that they'd used the water for the same purpose. They'll insist, "I heated the water a few minutes ago, but if you say you did, then it's obvious you imagine things. Perhaps you want coffee because you saw me having it."

This might sound funny, but it works like magic, and as time goes on, the victim's self-belief is depleted gradually, until the final stage where it dies.

27. Gaslighting at Work

Gaslighting knows no bounds, and you can find yourself being gaslighted at your workplace, either by your boss or a co-worker. Most times, perpetrators use it as a tactic to gain or maintain power, but that's not to say that it can't drive the victim crazy. For example, you were given a particular task, and you'd put in so much of your time; however, when you approached your boss, his response was, "But I told you to X instead, why did you waste your time doing this?

Considering the amount of time you've put into the work and the fact that you're sure you did what you were asked to do, you might get a little agitated and even try to be on the defensive. However, you might get a typical response like, "Are you sure you're not over-reacting?"

Or let's say your boss promises to give you a raise if certain conditions are met, and as a dedicated worker, you even exceed those conditions. However, when you bring the matter to his notice, he responds, "I did not promise to give you a raise. I only said I might consider giving you a raise if you met certain conditions, and so far, you've not met any."

Let's say you have a co-worker jostling to get promoted ahead of you and decides to gaslight you. From time to time, you'll realize that they'll say certain things specifically meant to undermine your self-confidence and even make you doubt your worthiness. For example, "Someone said that the director isn't impressed with the report you submitted. Trouble is looming." "Weren't you selected to join the team? Well, I figure you're not good enough to join." "Why are you mad at me? I only said you need to improve your skills."

Gaslighting from abusers isn't limited to words; sometimes, it comes with actions too. For example, you've spent most of your day working on a file on your computer. So, you decide to step out to get some air, but when you get back, you realize that the project has been mildly edited; however, you're confused because you're not sure whether you did it yourself.

Gaslighting is all about perpetuating confusion and insecurities in the victims' lives, and there are a plethora of ways to go about it.

28. Gaslighting in the Family

As explained, gaslighting describes a deadly form of psychological abuse. The methods used are subtle. Thus, victims are always unaware, and the end product is the distortion of their self-belief and self-confidence. Gaslighting is used by people of different origin, race, religions and even ethnic affiliations. It is also used by friends, lovers, co-workers, bosses, students and family members.

In the family setting, some narcissistic parents use gaslighting techniques to manipulate their children, which destroys their mental development. When children are manipulated into believing that their instincts are wrong all the time, they learn not to trust themselves. Narcissistic parents groom their children to lack any sort of belief in their sense of reality.

It is sad when you think of the thousands of children who depend on their narcissistic parents for teachings and support, only to poison and hinder their development and reality. They constantly seek validation and approval from other people because their instincts and individual voices were silenced years ago.

Whenever they think about themselves, rather than having feelings of internal strength and a strong sense of self, it always results in internal criticism and belittlement. The internal criticism results from the abuse they had suffered at the hands of their narcissistic parent as kids. Even when they have recurring thoughts, they might see it as "being stupid" or from upset, sad or angry. They may believe they are undeserving of these emotions or even "overreacting."

They have been gaslighted to believe they're always wrong. Thus they doubt their very own perception of the world. The saddest part of the situation is that they see nothing wrong in handling things and their entire thought process. They cannot differentiate their genuine thoughts from their projected ways of reasoning.

Chapter 10:
Stop the Narcissism

Dealing with a narcissist is incredibly difficult in the best of times, but there are many different ways to manage your relationship. Regardless of whether you are interested in severing all ties for good or are in a position to continue some degree of contact with a narcissist, understanding some of the ways to deal with the narcissist's toxic behaviors can help you minimize your risks of harm and abuse. You can also cause the narcissist to lose interest in you and move on to other targets when you prove yourself invulnerable to his manipulative tactics.

Consider each method carefully to decide if it meets your needs and helps you, and once you have chosen a strategy, remember to keep it up. No matter how much the narcissist may push and try to get your attention back, be consistent and get the best effect from your actions. None of these methods is easy, and each will take a tremendous amount of effort. Still, when you finally make it to the other side and realize how very free you are from the narcissist's abuse, you will recognize that it was worth every ounce of effort you put into it.

29. Cutting off the Narcissist

The easiest way to avoid harm from a narcissist is to end the relationship entirely. Refuse to engage in the relationship at all costs. Taking a huge step back from the relationship may be necessary so you can clear your head and see things for what they are. This is typically a permanent change and the only surefire way to ensure that the narcissistic abuse stops. If you refuse to play the game, the narcissist cannot manipulate you.

Furthermore, by refusing any engagement or communication with the narcissist, you can deny the narcissist's strongest motivator: your attention. You suddenly remove yourself as a reliable source of narcissistic supply, and if you continue to deny the narcissist, ultimately, he will have to go elsewhere to meet his need.

Keep in mind that when you do this, there will be a period called an extinction burst by psychologists. Consider an experiment in which a rat is taught to press a button to get a tiny nibble of candy. The rat very quickly learns to expect that candy every time the button is pressed, and the behavior of pressing a button becomes positively reinforced. The rat does this to get the sweet and does so repeatedly. If the rat goes up and presses the button and one day, it just stops giving out candy, and the rat will be confused. It will encourage the button repeatedly, with increasing enthusiasm, as it desperately tries to force it to do what was expected and provide more candy. Over time, the rat will lose interest when it becomes clear there is no further reaction, but it will go back to the button occasionally and try to press the button.

30. Take a Break from the Relationship

Similar to cutting off the narcissist, taking a break from the relationship involves a refusal to communicate. In this case, however, it is not permanent. The suspension is intended to allow you to clear your head and reevaluate whether you want to continue. Regardless of what he may accuse you of, remind yourself that this is not a punishment. You did not make this decision to hurt him; you made it protect and care for yourself. You are entitled to controlling who you communicate with, and if you decide that you do not want to talk to the narcissist, you are within your rights to make that choice.

When taking a break, it is appropriate to tell the person and to discuss things when you are ready. You do not have to provide him with a timeline, no matter how much he may bug you for one, and at that point, you can refuse all future contact. You are giving yourself the chance to cool off. Ensure that you do not say something that will make the situation worse or inflame the narcissist into doing something harmful.

Do not let the narcissist goad you into accusations of abuse or playing the victim. You are making a choice that works for you, and ultimately that is the essential part. You need the breathing room, and you are taking it. Remind yourself that you owe it to yourself to care for yourself, especially when no one else will. You cannot care for others if you are not caring for yourself.

31. Healthy Boundaries

Sometimes, cutting off a narcissist is not a viable option, and that is okay. When you have no choice but to continue contact, such as if bound by a court order to continue a co-parenting relationship, or you work with the narcissist and are not in a position to leave your job, you can focus on mitigating as much harm as possible and protecting yourself from the toxicity the narcissist seems to exude naturally.

Healthy boundaries are the most straightforward techniques to minimize harm from a narcissist, but they are difficult. These boundaries represent a line between what is acceptable and unacceptable, and they are to be set at your prerogative.

When the narcissist challenges a boundary, give him one warning. Tell him that if he continues to test your limits, you will provide a consequence. Tell the narcissist what that consequence for stomping on your boundary is, and every time it is done, you need to enforce the result. If you tell the narcissist that you will take an extended break if your boundary is broken, follow through on it. If you tell him you will stop talking if he calls you names in anger, you must immediately disengage and walk away. The key here is to follow through with the natural consequence, no matter how much the narcissist may cry, beg, or threaten.

32. Disengage

Disengaging does not mean ignoring or bottling your feelings, however. When you acknowledge what was said and give it the consideration it deserves, which is, admittedly, very little, this can be particularly difficult if the narcissist is a loved one you trusted, but remember to disregard his emotional reactions to the words that protect you. You do not fall into the narcissist's trap, and you do not let the narcissist regain control over your emotions, and in return, the narcissist will slowly lose interest.

33. The Grey Rock Method

Similar to disengaging emotionally, the grey rock method involves minimizing emotional reactions, but in this case, it is ignoring all interactions, both good and bad. Aim to avoid as much interaction as possible, and when you are forced to interact, keep it boring and meaningless. The name alludes to a grey rock on the side of the road. Consider how often you notice and remember all of the rocks you walk past in a given day—the answer is most likely none. People do not pay attention to something as mundane and worthless as a grey rock on the side of the road. Your goal in this method is to be as ordinary and useless to the narcissist as the grey rock. If you can achieve this state of mediocrity, the narcissist will slowly lose interest in you.

The trick is to be robotic in your responses. No matter how angry you may feel in response to whatever was said, respond in as few words as possible, and make sure it is never immediately after the message was sent (if it does not warrant an immediate response). For example, imagine that he messaged you saying that you are beautiful and he loves you. This should be ignored. Five minutes later, he messages asking how your shared child is doing. Give him the bare minimum answer while still being comprehensive. List what she is doing, whether she is sick, and maybe what she ate for dinner, but keep the interaction as emotionless as possible. Do not emote, no matter how tempting it may be.

34. Be Realistic

Keeping your interactions with the narcissist realistic will keep you from setting up high standards that she will never meet. Telling yourself that she will never be emotionally supportive and lacks empathy will help you keep reality in mind when dealing with a narcissist. If you are fully prepared for the narcissist to respond in a typical fashion, you will always be prepared, no matter how she responds, and you may even find that you are surprised upon occasion. This is key when maintaining a relationship with a narcissist, whether romantic, platonic, workplace, familial, or co-parenting. You are protected from the disappointment of narcissistic behavior.

35. Focus on the Positive

Likewise, when interacting with a narcissist, remembering to focus on the positive helps you recognize things that you enjoy about the person. After all, something must have attracted you to the narcissist at some point, and you may be happy to see tiny semblances of that person in the narcissist in front of you. While the personality is still likely vastly different from the one you met at first, there still may be parts of the narcissist that at least make her tolerable.

For example, she may be horrible at emotional support or anything but being the center of attention. Still, she may also genuinely be a good cook, and she loves to entertain all of your friends, or she may be brilliant. You enjoy the intellectual conversations you have over coffee, even if they involve occasional snide comments about how you do not understand because are not educated. Reminding yourself of the positives helps when you are ready to lose your temper with the narcissist, as outbursts would be detrimental.

36. Decide Your Hill to Die On

The last vital tactic to remember is to choose your hill to die on wisely. This is a fancy way of saying choose your battles carefully. Though narcissists seek out confrontation-avoidant people on purpose, avoiding conflict can prevent detection. For this reason, you always pick your battles wisely and be prepared to engage in a match only if you genuinely want to deal with the aftermath.

While some things are worthy of a dispute, such as a co-parent choosing to drive with children in the car while drunk, an argument over who said something first is petty, and the narcissist is not likely ever to concede or admit that he is lying. For this reason, only choose battles if you are willing to fight them. If you are unwilling to deal with the aftermath and ultimately do not bother fighting over it, whatever the narcissist did is insignificant.

Chapter 11:
A Hidden Narcissist Suffers Internally?

Narcissists are continuously overlooked for their good characteristics. Yet, they are vulnerable people who need understanding. They create their model through others and require self-identity when isolated. They are usually scared of getting a proper study of their behavior because the consequences would be frightening. Many are spiritually wasted, so they must explore getting support from another person. When describing a narcissist, you will see an egotistic character with an overblown personality. In reality, they depend on others for their thinking and attitudes.

Their thinking is defined by anxiety, uncertainty, and delusions. The unenthusiastic victim leaves them weak, helpless and hurt. They visualize themselves as a higher being, and when it is evident, it is impossible to live with.

Narcissistic behaviors are based on certain mindsets and beliefs that associate power with others' ill-treatment. This belief system makes narcissists view their peers as weak and inferior those do not need any attention. A narcissist person also believes that a person's worth is derived from his superiority or inferiority. These attributes are exhibited through emotions like rage and anger.

The mentality of a narcissist can cause him to detach from the feelings of others. It explains why most narcissists will never connect with the pain and challenges of their peers or relations. It also explains why they will always dismiss their complaints.

In the mind of a narcissist, a partnership does not need to exist in relationships. To him, any relationship must have a top dog and an underdog. The narcissist will continuously fight to be superior or the top dog. The general belief is that human beings can either rule or be ruled. Such a mentality causes narcissists to feel entitled to a certain kind of treatment.

Another mindset assumed by narcissists is that people are only there to serve their needs. They ignore others' needs because they think others do not need comfort and assistance. To them, it is the responsibility of their partners to serve and provide comfort. The narcissist wants to be adored, praised, and valued all the time.

In a nutshell, life with a narcissist is all about competition. Narcissists will compete with their colleagues, family members, and partners to ensure they remain in control. Due to this, narcissists never rest. They stay on the offensive to keep others admiring their courage. Their behavior revolves around building their status and interests.

Here is the thought pattern of a narcissist who is wired differently. Some of the common thoughts that keep running through their mind are:

· 'Why am I not getting the attention I need?'

· I only need to concentrate on myself and take care of my own needs.'

· I need to get out of this relationship because I do not feel in control.

· I am always right, you are always wrong, and you can do nothing about this fact.

· Why do I need to feel bad for someone else?

· I deserve some appreciation. Why have I not received it?

· I feel bored; it's time to stir things up.

· Why do you think you are to cause me shame?

Narcissists will avoid every activity or behavior that make their codependents feel appreciated. Their strategies are fashioned towards tearing others down. For a narcissist, there is the only method of winning – controlling the minds of other people. Sadly, with all the attention and admiration they receive, they rarely get pleased. They only feel suitable for a short while, then get back to doing hurtful things to remain in dominance. That is why most of them stay miserable for a good part of their lives.

Chapter 12:
The Narcissist's Target

Narcissists are emotional predators, and the fact that you're a human makes you automatically vulnerable to their antics. That said, it makes sense to identify the traits that narcissists identify in their targets, especially when you realize that you are being targeted for exploitation.

When you consider these traits, you'll realize how wonderful they are, especially if allowed to blossom in a healthy and loving relationship. Sadly, a narcissist will only use them to manipulate, exploit and damage their victims. Below are some of the traits that narcissists look out for in their potential victims:

1. Conscientiousness

2. Empathy

3. Integrity

4. Resilience

5. A high degree of sentimentality

37. Conscientiousness

Many people do not realize this, but one of the prime qualities a narcissist seeks is his potential victim's ability to be conscientious. Conscientious people are always concerned about others' wellbeing and carry out their obligations to others. They are vulnerable to narcissists because their decisions are tied to their conscience. Sadly, they project their sense of morality onto the narcissist, assuming he will do the same.

They know that a conscientious person is one of the very few people that would grant them numerous chances, give them the benefit of the doubt, and even care more about them than their personal needs.

Narcissists love to target conscientious people for romantic relationships because they know that moral people see caretaking as an obligation, especially in relationships. They know that these people are ready to fulfil their obligations even if they feel endangered or if it puts them in harm's way.

38. Empathy

Every narcissist's joy is to encounter an empathic victim because narcissists, in general, do not get a constant narcissistic supply (attention, praise, resources, etc.) from people who lack empathy - like themselves. Thus, the importance of securing a narcissistic target cannot be overemphasized.

Narcissists cannot show empathy towards others, but they carefully target people who have a great deal. The physical and emotional validation that empathic people give narcissists helps maintain their bloated ego and feelings of authority; otherwise, they practically starve and renew their hunt for a new supply source.

When you take everything into consideration, you'll realize that empathic people are the opposite of narcissists, and their attitude helps to empower narcissists in their abuse cycle. For example, the fact that an empath is always willing to see the narcissist's perspective even in the height of abuse maintains the abuse cycle repeatedly. As if that is not enough, narcissists identify with empathic people because they know that they're the ideal audience for their pity ploys even after highly abusive incidents.

If you happen to be an empathic person, understand that narcissists believe they can just put out a faux apology or create a sob story to write off their abuse. They do this because they know you'll always try to see reasons behind their toxic behaviors and even make excuses on their behalf.

They depend on your God-given ability to forgive and sympathize with them, irrespective of the ill-treatments they've subjected you to in the past. Most times, narcissists can escape retribution and accountability for their actions because they appeal to their victims' empathy.

It is tough to pretend to be someone you are not, and as such, empathic people constantly second-guess their decisions to punish narcissists for their actions because they feel an unbearable amount of guilt when they see the narcissist being prosecuted (either by society or law). Thus, they are inclined to protect their abusers instead of exposing them to the world.

39. Integrity

This might sound very funny, but narcissists are incredibly attracted to people who keep to their words. For example, if it is not a moral code to cheat or give up on a relationship prematurely, who stands to benefit?

The narcissist, who is morally and mentally impoverished! While the victims feel morally apprehensive about betraying the relationship, retaliation, or even withdrawing from their supposed obligations to the narcissists, the narcissist in question maintains zero remorse for harming their victims.

The victim possesses a rare gift that benefits them and their partners in a healthy and productive relationship. However, this same gift becomes a weapon in the hands of a narcissist – a deadly weapon used to destroy their self-worth and self-belief.

40. Resilience

The most painful part about being a victim of narcissistic abuse is realizing that you weren't wrong most times. As a victim of narcissistic abuse, your ability to bounce back from your abuser's cruel acts is something that strengthens your bond with him.

Resilience is an excellent quality to possess, especially when faced with adversities of life. Still, in an abusive relationship, the victim's resilience is exploited and used against him/her to keep them enslaved in the web of deceit and manipulation.

Even though resilient people are more aware of the dangers, they still find it challenging to give up on their abusers even after multiple abuse incidents. Typically, they will choose to disregard their instincts and fight for the relationship, assuming the role of a "fighter" or "savior," as they put in the energy to keep an unsustainable relationship afloat.

The saddest part about the resilient victim is that there are times when they even quantify their love by the amount of abuse they've suffered at the hands of their abuser. Unknown to them, this occurs because they have successfully developed an abusive bond with their toxic and offensive partner.

41. High Sense of Sentimentality

There is no gainsaying that narcissists are overbearing, petty, and manipulative. Thus, sentimental targets capable of falling deeply in love are incredibly appealing to narcissists because they know they can use love-bombing (extreme praise and flattery to groom a victim) to manipulate them easily. During the early stages of narcissistic relationships, narcissists shower their victims with so much love and attention; the idea is to secure their trust, and in this case, appeal to their craving for love. It is a strategy that works very well! They intentionally create sweet memories they want their victims to romanticize during future periods of abuse.

Narcissists love to play with their victim's emotions; they know they can get their victims hooked before they start to withdraw by creating a fraudulent "soulmate" effect that will cripple their victims and leave them wanting things to be as they were during the early stages of the relationship.

Narcissists find it very easy to trick empathic and sentimental people. The only thing they do is to fraud their victims into believing they're kicking off a meaningful, long-term relationship. Mind you, it is very typical for people to want to maintain long-term, healthy relationships, but it becomes a problem when a predatory narcissist is involved.

42. Why did the narcissist target you?

You have something the narcissist wants (lifestyle, power, money, position). In a narcissistic relationship, certain things come into play. First of all, it begins with a hook – a dream, most times. You think it is all about you and your wellbeing, by the truth is that the narcissist is all about control.

There are occasions where the narcissist will appear to be helpful, but when things don't go as planned, the tables will turn on you. However, when you realize the pattern and opt to hold him accountable for his actions, things get out of hands and degenerate rapidly.

Chapter 13:
Narcissist and Relationships

43. Charming You

During the charming phase, the narcissist will set you up as an ideal person that everyone should strive to get to know. Through intense observation, they will figure out just what you desire in a relationship. Then in a brief time, they prove to you that they are all you have been looking for and more. They lay on the charm fast and quick by love-bombing you.

Is there something you've always wanted to do but have never gotten around to? They will make it happen. Is there some need you have that you've always wished could be fulfilled? They're going to take care of it ASAP. At first blush, the narcissist seems to be everything you have ever wanted. But that's not true. They're only assuming a persona that matches all you've sought in a relationship. This persona will be discarded when they feel they've got you to hook, line, and sinker.

44. Making you feel worthless

The narcissist will make you feel like your life has no meaning. She does this without fail. It's the next thing to expect after she has spent such a short time loving you a little too intensely. Once they've got you believing that they are the one you've waited for your whole life, what happens next? They proceed to yank the rug out from underneath your feet. Next thing you know, this very same person who was full of praise and worship for you will take every chance she can to make you feel like crap. It's a bait and switch situation.

Now you find yourself wondering what happened to the person you got to know at the start of the relationship. Where did they go? They have got to be there somewhere. Perhaps they are only going through a rough patch, so you do anything and everything within your power to regain their approval and love, hoping that a change in your attitude and behavior will be enough to bring them back, so you can continue to enjoy their attention and love.

45. Hogging the Conversation

Where you used to be the star of the relationship, that changes. The narcissist will supplant you and become the only one worthy of note. All conversation becomes strictly about the narcissist. Otherwise, it's not worth engaging in. For the narcissist, it is delightful to watch your frustration as whatever attention you used to enjoy from him is consistently being taken away, and more importantly, given to him instead. It's a thrilling power move for the narcissist you have the great misfortune of dating.

46. Violating your Boundaries

The narcissist will be completely aware of things you do not take lightly and decide that those are the exact things she's going to mess with. She will watch as you grow incredibly frustrated with her. She will enjoy the constant emotional rollercoaster you put her through, as she convinces you she never meant to hurt your feelings.

The truth is that the narcissist has been out for blood since day one. She wants to hurt your feelings. This is how she controls you. She wants to watch as the so-called "boundaries" you have set up for yourself are slowly but surely eroded by the sheer force that she is. It's a game, and it's intoxicating for her to watch you become a shadow of yourself.

47. Breaking the Rules

In line with testing your boundaries and pushing past them, the narcissist will break the rules. They know that certain things are a no-no for you, but they will go right ahead and do stuff they know you disagree with anyway.

You and the narcissist could have a conversation about something they did, and they will agree with you that, yes, they ought never have behaved that way. But guess what happens after a few days or weeks? The narcissist goes right back to doing the same things — but worse. Why does he do this? He knows that constantly breaking the rules is a surefire way to hurt you in the end. He knows that this is the best way to program you to be okay with his games.

48. Changing You

When you begin dating the narcissist, be careful if your friends and family constantly talk about the fact that you're changing, and not in a good way. The fact that they're able to tell you this is a good thing; it means your narc lover has not yet completed her mission of isolating and walling you off from the people who love you.

49. Negative Emotions and Feedback

Dating a narc never feels good. It's like you're caught in a tsunami of negative emotions. You have to deal with their insecurities, their manipulative lies, and their general awfulness. At some point, you'll begin to wonder whether or not you're good enough as a human being. This is the natural thing to do because the person who once thought the world of you now feels that you leave much to be desired and aren't doing your best to be better. Whatever that means.

50. Making Everything Your Fault

In a relationship with a narcissist, you're going to find that you're somehow always causing trouble. That's how devastating the narcissist can be when you are in a relationship with her. At no point is the narcissist going to accept responsibility for whatever it is they have done. All their actions and words are going to be on your shoulders.

If you had not been a certain way or had simply gone along with everything they told you, everything from A to Z would not have happened. I recall my mother once telling me that I was responsible for all the evil in the world. I wanted to ask her how back then, as it made no sense to my innocent, child-like mind. Now I understand that for the narcissist, logic is overrated. It doesn't need to make sense. If they say such and such is like so and so because of you, it simply is.

Chapter 14:
Empathy

Ask yourself the following questions to determine if you're an empath:

• Can you perceive people in some way?

• Do you feel people's emotions and mistake them for yours?

• Can you think along the same line as other people?

• Do your feelings change as soon as you meet a particular person?

• Do you sometimes wonder whether you're co-dependent, neurotic, or even crazy?

• Can you read peoples' minds?

It can be awesome having the ability to pick up on other people's energies. Still, it can be a real struggle on the downside when the said energies are dark, especially if the empath in question knows nothing of their ability.

As an empath, these are some traits that you're bound to display:

Highly Sensitive

People keep on telling you that you're too sensitive. This is because what they say or do affects you easily. You can read into their unsaid messages when they talk or do something. This sensitivity can make you susceptible to things that don't hurt well-adjusted people. Your high sensitivity makes you give a lot of thought to what you do or say. This pattern always leads to self-inhibiting tendencies. You end up customizing yourself too much so that the world can fall in love with you. The habit of suppressing your genuine emotions comes with a cocktail of challenges.

Soak Up Other Peoples' Energies

You could be having a fantastic day with your spirits high, and then you go to Starbucks and sit next to a family who, unbeknownst to you, just lost one of their members. Nothing is said. All are sipping at their coffee with quiet faces. Ever so slowly, the joy you first had begins to fade away, and in its place, sadness takes over. You have no reason to be sad, but you experience this sadness anyway. Soon, the family gets up, troops out of Starbucks, and then your sadness fades away. You had just absorbed their energies.

Introverted

Being introverted is not the same as being shy. A shy person might loathe being alone and feel rejected for a lack of human contact, but on the other hand, an introvert gets drained when they stay too long with other people, and they cherish being alone. A shy person has self-inhibiting tendencies, but an introvert has a strong sense of self and stays true. Empaths are more likely to be introverted than extroverted. They don't shun all human contact but prefer socializing on one-on-one terms or within small groups.

Highly Intuitive

One of the most effective weapons in an empath's hands is their gut feeling. They can sniff out the true nature of a situation. This makes it a bit hard to play games with an empath. They will see right through your tricks. As an empath, if you meet someone, you tend to have a gut feeling of what that person is really like. You are always in tune with your surroundings and can tell when there's danger.

Overwhelmed By Relationships

Conventional relationships spend as much time together as possible. An empath cannot thrive in this kind of arrangement because they constantly pick up on their partner's emotions and mistake them as their own. This is not to say that empaths cannot form any relationships. However, the traditional relationship needs to be deconstructed. For instance, they can have a room of their own that they may retreat to when their urge to be alone kicks in, and also, their partners should be patient with them.

Take Long To Process Emotions

The average person has laser attention on their emotions. Whether sadness or joy, it kicks in suddenly. Their emotional reflexes are fast too. An empath takes the time to understand the feelings they are currently feeling. For instance, if something terrible goes down, the sadness won't register immediately. They will first try to process the situation, going over the details time and again, and then the sadness will accumulate inside. They can experience emotions in such a powerful way. Thus, whether it's sadness or joy, they feel it completely.

Love Nature

Most empaths are at their happiest when surrounded by nature. Whether it's the sunlight kissing their skin, the rain falling on them, or taking in a gulp of fresh air, no other activity restores their balance as much as being surrounded by the natural world. They feel a deep sense of connection with nature. When an empath is experiencing a tsunami of emotions, one of the therapeutic measures would be taking a stroll through an open area beneath the sky.

Strong Senses

An empath boasts of very developed senses. They can catch the slightest whiff of an odor, see into the shadows, hear the tiniest sound, and feel the vibrations of various other things. These developed senses make them really good at noticing the small stuff. Empaths seem to see what would ordinarily escape the attention of most people. For this reason, they tend to flourish in careers that demand close attention and the exploration of the abstract.

Generous

There isn't a more selfless person than an empath. They don't have to have something to help. For instance, when an empath comes across a street child and sees her suffering, it tugs at their heart. They want to give her some food and find a way of removing her from the streets. The majority of the world doesn't care about street children and sees them as an annoyance. We assume that the world's empaths play a critical role in helping street children and other people experiencing hardship.

Creative

Empaths tend to be very creative. This is aided by the wealth of emotions they are constantly experiencing. Their creative nature manifests itself in almost every aspect of their life — food, relationships, homes, and most importantly, one's career. An empath is likely to do well in the arts. They have tremendous potential when it comes to drawing, writing, singing, or making films. They tend to portray their emotions unambiguously and can capture the feelings of other people as intended.

People are Drawn to You

If an empath isn't aware of their unique gift, they are likely to hide from the world. They would rather hide and be safe than stay among people and experience every emotion imaginable. This can make society grow suspicious and even hate them. However, if an empath is self-aware and knows of their ability to soak up the energies floating around them, then people will be drawn to them. People know that empaths have a tremendous capacity to understand and help them get through whatever challenges they are facing.

Empaths Fall into the Following Distinct Categories:

• Geomantic empaths: These empaths are tuned to a particular environment or landscape. Geomantic empaths are connected to specific sites like buildings, lakes, oceans, and mountains. These empaths feel the historical emotions of these sites. For instance, if an empath visits an area where people were slaughtered many years, they can still feel the sorrow. Empaths attach feelings to different environments so that each setting evokes certain emotions. Such empaths tend to carry souvenirs to remind them of various backgrounds.

• Physical empaths: Also known as medical empaths, they pick up on the condition of someone else's body. They instinctively know what ails another person. In extreme cases, they can pick up on the symptoms to share in the other person's pain. Physical empaths also have healing abilities. They tend to take careers in conventional or alternative medicine. Physical empaths are great at taking care of unhealthy people. Those who have ailments trust them instinctively because they feel that they care.

• Emotional empaths: They are sensitive to the emotional energy floating around them. As an emotional empath, you will absorb other people's emotions and think they are yours. This can be deeply distressing if you're constantly around negative people. An emotional empath should increase their self-awareness to distinguish their emotions from those of others. Emotional empaths tend to withdraw from other people so they can spend time alone and recharge. An emotional empath should protect their energy by following various healing practices.

• Animal empaths: You have certainly seen someone in your neighborhood who is more interested in keeping company with animals than humans. They have a specific pet or even various pets that mean the world to them. There's a high likelihood that such a person is an animal empath. An animal empath feels a deep connection with animals. They sense what the animals want, and the animals love them back. The link is so deep that they have a way of communicating with each other. An animal empath answers to their intense desire to connect by domesticating their animals of choice. Also, they tend to be passionate about animal rights and contribute to funds that advance animal welfare.

• Plant empaths: A plant empath shares a deep connection with a particular plant or plants in general. The plant evokes certain emotions when they touch it. A plant empath can communicate with the plant and know its condition. They like hanging out near the plant in a natural environment, bringing it into their house or planting it in the garden.

• Precognitive empaths: Are you the type of person who can always tell the future? And this is not for you alone, but also for unrelated people or events? You're certainly a precognitive empath. You tend to "see" things before they come to pass. Your visions are made manifest in various ways, such as dreams or feelings. Having this ability to foresee the future is both rewarding and distressing. It can help you brace for the future, and at the same time, it can amplify your misery, knowing the pain that awaits.

Chapter 15:
Co-dependency and Narcissists

Codependency and narcissism are two sides to the same coin. They both lack a healthy sense of self and struggle with defining who they are, bringing a whole barrage of issues to the table. Ultimately, codependency and narcissism are two different reactions to similar situations. Whereas the narcissist learns to be overtly selfish, the codependent learns to be overtly selfless. However, they are not always strictly opposites. In some cases, the two can overlap to some degree; someone can exhibit codependent behaviors in certain situations while behaving narcissistically in other contexts. For example, someone could be very codependent in a marriage or relationship, seeking to cater to their spouse's every whim, but be quite narcissistic with other people, such as friends or strangers. Though narcissism and codependence are both quite different, their root cause is the same.

51. What is Co-dependency?

In many normal relationships, we develop dependent relationships. This means that we prioritize our partners and rely on each other for love and support. The connection is mutually beneficial, and neither person worries about expressing their genuine emotions. In a dependent relationship, both people enjoy time spent away from the relationship while still meeting the other's needs.

However, in a codependent relationship, the codependent feels that his only worth comes from being needed. He will make huge sacrifices, martyring himself to ensure the other person's needs are met. He exists solely for the relationship and feels as though he is worthless outside of that relationship. The association is with his only identity, and he will cling to it at all costs; within that relationship, he will ignore his own needs and wants, feeling they are unimportant.

52. Causes of Co-dependency

Like NPD, many external factors are believed to cause a codependent personality to develop. This is because both codependency and narcissism are similar personality flaws, stemming from the exact root cause of damaged self-esteem.

53. Poor Parental Relationships

Frequently, people who have developed a codependent personality have grown up repeatedly having conflicts with their parents throughout their childhood. Their parents may have prioritized themselves or somehow otherwise denied that the child's needs were essential. By constantly downplaying his needs, the child internalizes that those needs are not important. After all, if the child's parents could not be bothered to tend to them, they must not matter.

The child learns to prioritize his or her parents instead and feels greedy or selfish when committing to self-care. Frequently, this kind of relationship between parent and child happens because they have an addiction problem and will do anything to feed the addiction. The parent never matured past the selfish development stage as a child and focuses solely on him or herself. Because of all the time spent focusing on the parent's needs, the child never develops the independence and identity necessary to succeed in life. Feeling incomplete when not needed, these people frequently seek out other enablers that allow them to continue living in this fashion.

54. Living with Someone Dependent on Care

When a child grows up around someone else who requires regular or around-the-clock care beyond the realm of the normal, whether due to severe illness, injury, or some sort of mental illness, the child's needs go unmet in favor of meeting more pressing ones. The child is pushed aside in favor of the person who needs care, and the child's needs become less essential to internalize. The child may also consider the dependent person who is causing his needs to be put on the back burner as he takes care of someone who literally cannot care of herself.

Living with a family member who requires extra care does not necessarily cause codependency to develop, and many people make it through the caregiving stage without issue. But certain personality types are predisposed to codependent tendencies. It becomes an issue if the young child is dependent on care, and the parent tends to focus entirely on the dependent person instead of spending the time the child needs to grow and thrive.

55. Abuse

It is no surprise that abuse, whether physical, emotional, or sexual, leaves lasting harm on a child. While some children go on to abuse others, others fall into a pattern of codependency. A child exposed to repeated abuse eventually begins to develop a coping mechanism to suppress her feelings. This leaves her only caring about other people's needs while neglecting her own.

Abuse victims also tend to seek out people with similar tendencies as the abuser as this is what is familiar. They know how to live through the abuse and understand that the relationship will often revolve around codependent behaviors. Abusers and narcissists love codependents, as codependents tolerate vast amounts of abuse that would make other people baulk.

56. Key Features of Co-dependency

Frequently, codependency manifests itself in incredibly recognizable ways. Though every person is different, and behaviors will change depending on the relationship, there are several patterns associated with codependency. Knowing how to identify these will enable you to recognize when you or someone you know is exhibiting codependent tendencies. If you feel that you may be codependent, seeking a trained psychologist's professional opinion would be a great place to start your journey toward understanding yourself.

· Exaggerated sense of responsibility: Codependents frequently feel as though the weight of their loved one's actions is on their shoulders.

· Confuse love and pity

· Doing more than their fair share

· Sensitive when good deeds are unrecognized: When a codependent feels as though her efforts have gone ignored, she is likely to feel hurt or as she is not good enough. She will try to martyr herself further to get the recognition she craves to soothe her low self-esteem and prove that she matters.

· Feeling guilty when caring for self: Any time the codependent engages in acts she sees as selfish or unnecessary in the grand scheme of things, she will feel guilty. After all, her needs should be met last, and if she does anything other than that, she is behaving selfishly, which is unacceptable.

· Rigid: Codependents do not tolerate change. They often seek out familiar things for this reason, which leads them to constantly seek out other enablers in relationships, even if these enablers prove to be abusive.

· Cannot set healthy boundaries: Codependents see no boundaries between themselves and their enablers. They have no sense of self outside the relationship or apart from the enabler. Because they fail to set boundaries, the relationship eventually consumes their lives and leaves little room for anything else. This lack of limits also leads to needs going unmet

· Needs recognition to feel whole: Without recognition for their good deeds and caring for others, codependents feel unwanted and unimportant. They require people to recognize their actions to help bolster their fragile self-esteem.

· Need to control others: Codependents, feeling utterly responsible for their enablers' actions, also seek some level of control over their relationships. Because codependents always do everything possible for the enablers, they develop the control they desire, and the enabler allows them to have it. Without power, the codependents feel unable to help.

· Fear of abandonment: With their subpar self-esteem and feeling as though they have no sense of identity beyond their relationships, codependents are terrified of being abandoned.

· Poor decision-making skills: Frequently, their dysfunctional opinion and view of their relationships make codependents opt for bad decisions. These could range from refusing to leave a dangerous situation because they want to stay with their partner or refuse to meet their needs, even if it makes them sick or hurt.

· Difficulty communicating: Codependents struggle to communicate their own needs and wants because they are so caught up in the idea that they do not matter. Even if they hate something, they will refuse to say it if they think it would be detrimental, even slightly, to the other person.

· Unhealthy dependence on relationship: Codependents exist solely for their relationships and enablers, and that dependence crosses the line into the territory of dysfunction.

· Untrusting: Frequently, due to so much dysfunction in childhood, codependents tend to distrust those around them, especially those who insist that their needs be met or they try to point out that their relationship is unhealthy.

· Confrontation-avoidant: Codependents avoid confrontation at all costs. They have developed a tendency to avoid their own needs to avoid confrontation, and that tendency has extended well into adulthood. The codependent will do anything to avoid conflict, especially with the enabler.

57. Co-dependents and Narcissists

As you read about codependents and their tendencies, it should have become evident that codependents make the narcissist's ultimate target. They meet every line on the narcissist's agenda in choosing a target, and they are the ultimate victim. In a partnership between a codependent and a narcissist, the codependent gives endlessly to the narcissist, who needs the attention to feel loved. The narcissist gets to provide the codependent with the gift of being needed.

Both the narcissist and the codependent get their dysfunctional needs met. While this may seem like the perfect arrangement, it still encourages two people to live incredibly unhealthy lives. The codependent never has her basic needs met and still has broken self-esteem and lack of identity. The narcissist never gives back in the relationship and believes the narcissist is the only one who matters.

The narcissist's self-esteem and disordered thinking are not fixed through being catered to. This leads to an interesting relationship in which both the narcissist and the codependent enable each other.

Chapter 16:
Dealing with a Narcissist

There is no more fabulous teacher than personal experience and the knowledge and awareness that comes with it. Cutting all contact with the narcissist is the best possible scenario and speeds up the healing process. However, most of the time, relationships are not so simple, and there are other people or factors involved, such as children, colleagues, shared property, the workplace or family members. Of course, narcissists can the parents of our children, siblings, or bosses; in spite of the need to minimize contact, we are forced to have encounters with them, sometimes daily.

58. Awareness

When you are aware of their selfish behavior and have figured out their patterns, you can use this awareness to your advantage. Once you see through the narcissist and accept who they are, you can predict their reactions and use that knowledge to manipulate the situation in your favor. This does not mean becoming a narcissist yourself. It simply means protecting yourself from the abuser by knowing how they abuse you. You know the narcissist is up for what they can get, and you know they never change. What can change is your approach. Study your narcissist, observe them and spot the behavioral scheme you see. Knowing how they work and understanding that they are a self-serving person with a cluster B disorder, incapable of empathy, won't directly change how they treat you very much. What will change is how you perceive and react to them. This will minimize the mental and emotional damage they can inflict. Nothing they do is ever about you or anyone else; it is always about them. Knowing and accepting this and changing or enlightening them will save you from future hurt and giving in to their games.

59. Passivity and Disengagement

Covert narcissists are never mindful of your needs, so trying to explain your point of view, communicate your feelings, or seek understanding will only give them more material to manipulate you with. Don't try to seek justice or share with them; there is no space for compromise, tolerance, or a peaceful resolution unless it suits them at the moment. The best way to actively handle their blame games and gaslighting is to be aware of them and play along. For instance, when they blame you for being selfish, just tell them, you are right; I am so selfish. I agree with everything you say. If they are trying to convince you that you have done something you know you haven't, just play along. Oh yes, you are right; I remember I did that. This way, you turn their weapons, gaslighting and manipulation, against them, as they are perfectly aware, just like you are, that you never did what they accused you of. A narcissist is not a healthy individual, and this inauthentic act can protect you from being controlled by them. In the process, always be mindful of your actions and know who you are dealing with to protect your integrity.

You can also do this when you notice their behavior makes you feel heavyhearted or hurt, simply by disengaging and detaching yourself from the situation. Part of the disengagement technique includes self-discipline. When something feels off, don't try to find out why: just distance yourself from the situation. A narcissist communicates from an ego-centered place, and asking for explanations will only bring you more confusion and headache. Trust that the very feeling that something is not right is enough for you to leave the situation. Do so by acting peacefully and kindly, without explaining yourself, so as not to give the narcissist space to pull you back into their drama.

60. Privacy protection

You are dealing with an individual who is demanding a lot of mindfulness. What gives narcissists their power to control their targets is knowing their targets, predicting their behaviors and being aware of what makes them tick. That is why protecting yourself from narcissistic abuse in the future means keeping your life as private as possible. Don't let them know how you feel, what you fear or what you hope for. Distance yourself as much as possible and don't get them involved in your life. This will create a necessary barrier as they can't manipulate your feelings when they don't know what matters to you. Keep the narcissist informed only of fundamental things, such as moving locations when still sharing custody over children or keeping it strictly professional in the workplace.

61. Self-empowerment

In the end, there is nothing that defeats the narcissist more and protects you from them than having firm personal boundaries. This is something you will find easier to do by the end of the third stage of healing, so be patient. These skills are built slowly and require some practice. While not an easy road, fighting narcissistic abuse teaches us to protect ourselves and prioritize our needs once we know it.

Developing skills to cope with narcissism in others also includes practicing self-awareness, understanding and accepting your vulnerability without feeling flawed or weak. Being vulnerable means being human. Leave no space for someone to devalue you. Don't be afraid to say, no, when things don't feel right. There is no need to explain yourself, especially when dealing with a covert narcissist. Assert your boundaries calmly and don't feel bad for doing so. Saying no isn't selfish: it is healthy. The narcissist will probably try to pull you into their drama, so be aware of guilt-tripping and stay strong in your integrity. Trust yourself enough to walk away from things that don't feel good. It is ok and healthy to put yourself first. It is ok not to respond when you don't feel like it. Love is never restricting or conditional. Love is not abuse. Love feels good.

Being open to love, being giving and helpful are great virtues and should be cherished. These virtues will help you create balanced, healthy relationships in the future with a healthy individual who can reciprocate your love equally. Narcissists don't know how to appreciate it, and they give themselves permission to take it for granted and misuse it, which is not your fault. Not everyone is worthy of your love, and no one should cost you your peace of mind.

You are loveable and you are strong; otherwise, you wouldn't be here. And you are much more than you were told you are. One day, you will make it through. Life will be much different, and a narcissist won't cause you pain anymore. Once you get there, just remember to give yourself credit for it. Through adversity, we grow.

Chapter 17:
Your Road to Recovery

One of the things that you have to realize is that a narcissist does not see the need to seek help from a therapist because they think there is nothing wrong with them. Recovery is for those who have been through abuse. If you have been in a relationship with a narcissist, it is high time you left and sought help from a professional. This kind of support is needed to rebuild your self-confidence and bounce back to your former self-esteem.

Here are some of the steps you will have to go through on your journey through healing to recovery:

62. Step 1: Cut contact

Once you have left the relationship, keep it at that! Stop maintaining contact with your abuser. The main reason why you left is that the situation was not working for you. Nothing will happen that can make things better. The best way to recover from abuse is to block all forms of communication.

If you have joint custody of your children, you may not be able to wipe this person entirely from your life. Therefore, it is advisable to create a strict custom contract, according to which you only communicate on matters regarding your children using third-party channels exclusively! Otherwise, ensure that you have set up court orders for all forms of agreements.

Remember that you lived with them, and so the narcissist knows your weak points and how they can wound you even more profoundly. It is not until we heal that we will stop forcing ourselves on the narcissist for love or craving them - or even justifying giving them a second chance. When we completely stop contact, we can truly begin to heal.

63. Step 2: Release that trauma so that you begin functioning again

If we are going to heal, we have to be willing to reclaim our power. We have to do the exact opposite of what we used to believe, "I can fix him/her, I will feel better." Your power belongs inside you. The moment you take your focus away from your abuser, you will be able to channel that power into rebuilding your self-love and paying closer attention to making yourself whole again.

At first, it might seem like understanding who a narcissist is and what they do is essential. But the truth is that these things cannot heal your internal trauma. You need to decide to let go of that horrific experience so you can be at peace. You will begin to rise, get relief and rebalance once you have decided to take your power where it belongs - inside you.

64. Step 3: Forgive yourself for what you have been through

When the insecure and wounded parts of us are still in pain, we often are pushed into behaving like damaged children. We are constantly looking for people's approval, especially from our abuser. In fact, we hand our abuser the power to treat us as they see fit. And that's the time when you will realize that you have given them all your resources:

money, time and health. The most unfortunate thing is that while doing that, you end up hurting the people that matter the most in your life…your children, siblings, parents, and friends.

You will realize that when you forgive yourself, you acknowledge that this was all a learning curve; hence, you will use the experience to reclaim your life. When you release your regrets and self-judgments, you can start setting yourself free to realize greatness in your life irrespective of what stage you are at. This is the point when you begin to feel hope again that will steer you forward and a life full of purpose.

65. Step 4: Release everything and heal all your fears of the abuser and what they might do next

Do you know what bait is to a narcissist? Anxiety, pain, and distress. These are the things that can perpetuate another cycle of abuse no matter how much we tell ourselves that we have separated from them. It is indeed true that abusers can be relentless. In most cases, they do not like being losers. They are not as powerful and impactful as you may have thought.

They need you to fear and go through pain to function. Once you have healed your emotional trauma, they fall apart. Therefore, you must become grounded and stoic by not feeding into their drama; this way, they will soon wither away along with their power and credibility.

66. Step 5: Release the connection to your abuser

So many people liken their freedom from a narcissist to that of exorcism. When we liberate ourselves from the darkness that filled our beings, we detox and let light and life come in. If that light has to take over the shade, the darkness has to leave to make space for something new to come in. In the same manner, you must release all the parts of you that were trapped by your abuser so you can tap into a more supernatural power - the power of pure creativity.

When you disentangle yourself from the narcissist, it is not just about cutting the cord; it is also about releasing all the belief systems you might have associated with subconsciously. It is only then that you can break free to be a new person and not a narcissist's target.

Even though it might be tempting to seek revenge on your abuser, this is something that you have to try hard to avoid. Rage has the power of pulling you back into deeper darkness and a game that your abuser is an expert at. The best form of revenge is the one in which you decide to take back your freedom and render your abuser irrelevant.

67. Step 6: Realize your liberation, truth, and freedom

Traditionally, we learn that loving ourselves is a very selfish act. However, when it comes to finding liberation from the hands of our abusers, the truth will set us free from captivity. Yes, it is challenging to do, but it is a necessary step toward freedom.

Society has taught us that we are treated by others the same way we treat them. However, this is a false premise because we are treated according to the way we treat ourselves. In other words, the measure of love we obtain from others is equivalent to what we feel about ourselves.

Therefore, when we open up to healing and recovery, we open the doors for others to love us in more healthy ways than ever before. This serves as a template by which we can teach our children not to carry around subconscious patterns of abuse passed on by our ancestors. This positive modeling only starts when we decide to take responsibility for our own happiness and freedom. We slowly see the change that we would wish to see when we let go of being someone's victim and stop handing other people our power.

68. So, what do you need to learn?

69. Refocus

One of the best things to learn from the whole experience is the danger of holding on to emotional attachments. When you let go, you experience the power that comes from healing. Take time to release those bond so you can refocus all your efforts on building a new life.

70. Self-confidence

If you want to live a life of greatness after your abuse, you must be willing to start putting your life back together. With self-confidence you can reclaim your old self and find an even higher power to steer you toward success and victory. Once you start experiencing self love, you will be able to turn a chaotic life into one laden with calmness and joy.

71. Mindfulness

One of the things that you need to learn is to be fully present in the moment where your mind is not anxious about anything. It's the moment when you are calm and have clarity of thought. Only then that can you learn some of the powerful tools and tricks that will lead you to a life full of purpose and adventure.

72. Authenticity and integrity

The good thing for most survivors of abuse is the fact that they are often sincere. Their actions and words usually line up well. Through this extraordinary quality, you recognize your real personality and live a life doing good deeds for the entire society. Although these qualities are things to be proud of, you have to be willing to protect yourself, knowing that the person receiving your good deed is capable of reciprocating.

73. Establish new, robust, and healthy relationships

One of the best things you can learn from abuse is the art of connecting with new people in new ways. The best way is to attract healthy relationships with authentic friends who offer you a support system. Learn how to handle triggers, anxieties, fears, and stress. When you gain healthy relationship skills, you will be empowered to make better and more informed decisions in the future.

74. Accountability for your actions

Unfortunately, your narcissistic partner does not possess this gift; hence, their actions often make you feel more vulnerable. However, gaining your freedom from a narcissist allows you to fortify and reclaim your power when going into new relationships with the knowledge of how to set boundaries and getting people to respect them, no matter what. This will pave the way for healthier relationships filled with love and esteem, whether at the workplace, in your family, or your personal life.

75. Willingness to transition your relationships into mature and fundamental levels of intimacy

The good thing about surviving abuse is that you are empathetic. In other words, you learn what it takes to experience a healthy relationship filled with love and care for the other person. It is with this understanding that you can now exercise self-awareness. At some level, you know that the infatuation you have about the past will fade, and you will get back up on your horse and work on gaining true intimacy. You will be interested in truly knowing the other person well on a deeper, more personal level so you can unravel their real personality.

As a survivor, you are better equipped to move past your pain and abuse to a healthy relationship, whether in your family, workplace or love life. You can only do this with the right person, one who can reciprocate on the same deep level of emotional vulnerability and build complete trust.

Chapter 18:
Long-Term Recovery

Healing doesn't end even after the narcissist has been removed from your life. It is a process that takes an immeasurable amount of time. Nurturing your recovery will enable you to continue down the path of health and happiness. To ensure that you heal in the best way possible and the pain doesn't come back, I provide a few more practical steps. The recovery process needs to be continually nurtured. It's not a weekend program you do and never think about again. The emotional pain might subside, but there will still be bumps in the road. It is not a climb up a mountain but rather a ride on a rollercoaster. If you learn to anticipate the highs and lows, it will be much easier to stay in control of your emotional management as you ride along.

76. Breathing Exercises

Anyone dealing with anxiety can benefit from learning a few breathing exercises. This is the first place your mind should go when you start to feel overwhelmed and panicked. Breathing exercises are just as important when you are feeling happy as well. We often forget to focus on breathing, exacerbating the body's already panicked state when under intense stress. If you feel like texting your narcissistic ex, are triggered by your surroundings, or simply want to feel a bit more peace, try some of these exercises:

Alternate nose breathing - Take your right hand and place your pinky gently on your left nostril until it is closed. Breathe in through the right nostril. Hold it for a beat, then place your thumb on your right nostril in the same fashion as you remove your pinky from your left nostril. Slowly let the air out. Alternate your hands and nostrils as you feel yourself become more relaxed.

4-7-8 Breathing - Breathe in as you count to four. Hold it as you count to seven. Breathe out as you count to eight. Take a few seconds in between before doing this exercise again. You will feel the euphoria take over your brain. If you think too lightheaded, wait at least ten minutes before trying again.

Alternate nose-mouth breathing: Breathe in only through your nose as you count to five. Breathe out through a small hole in your mouth as you count to ten. This is a fundamental exercise whenever you are feeling scattered.

77. Mindfulness

Mindfulness is the best tool to keep you grounded. One thought can quickly turn into 1,000 ideas in an hour if you let yourself sit there and dwell on it. The mind is constantly active, so you can't just turn it off. Even in dreams, you might have to deal with memories of the narcissist!

Think of your thoughts like a snowball rolling down a hill. At first, you might not notice them, and maybe you don't even think they are a big deal, but as a thought keeps rolling, it collects more and more snow until it becomes so big it could roll right over a house! Stop your thoughts with mindfulness as soon as you notice them moving.

Try these mindful activities to help keep your mind calm:

Pick a color: Think of a random color—whatever comes to your mind first. Notice everything in the room of the same color. If you find your mind slipping back into anxious thoughts, find another color and repeat as needed until you can distract yourself further or refocus your attention where it needs to go.

Five senses: Once your mind starts racing, pull it back in your control by finding an object to correspond with each of your reasons. For sight, notice a luscious plant. For sound, maybe spot a guitar or CD. For touch, identify something soft, rough, or textured. For smell, perhaps you notice a candle. For taste, you might pick out a candy dish. These things don't have to correspond with their obvious sense either. Think about what the leather couch smells like or what a houseplant tastes like. You don't have to do anything more than simply identify these things to keep your mind distracted.

78. Meditation

Meditation is like taking mindfulness to the next step. It involves refocusing your energy so your mind becomes completely blank. Search "guided meditation" on YouTube to find some beginner exercises if you are skeptical about meditation.

To begin, find a special place you can dedicate solely to meditative practices. This might include a sunroom, a backyard, or even a particular spot at the foot of your bed. Cleanse this space with sage to reset the energy. Sit in a comfortable position. You can sit in the classic meditative pose with the bottom of your feet placed together and your legs bent. You can also lie down with your eyes closed. Ensure you are in a comfy position that you won't want to move from repeatedly.

Start by focusing on your breathing. You can pick from any of the breathing exercises mentioned above. Pay attention to how your body feels as you breathe in and out. Notice any discomforts and try and relieve it from your body as you relax further.

As thoughts pass by, picture them as clouds. They will fade away and transform into shapes as you are lying there looking up at the sky. You can't grab them, you can't hold them, you can't change them. Just let them float away. Pay them no mind. They will keep coming, but you will keep letting them simply fade away.

Meditating can be hard for beginners. You might find that your mind is continually going back to scattered thoughts. New anxieties and big fears might come in like a blaring alarm. Remember to center back on your breathing. You don't have to give in to these thoughts or do anything with them. There is no urgency for reflection. The most important part of meditation is to clear your mind so you can reset your thoughts.

79. Creating

Creating anything can be incredibly fulfilling. Not everyone will be the next Picasso, but freely expressing yourself will help you become more comfortable. Finishing a craft project like a knitted scarf or refurbished chair can boost your self-esteem and give you something to be proud of.

Explore different creative avenues and find something you feel comfortable with. Try oil paints, acrylics, or watercolors. Try sketching with pencils, chalk, or even crayons. Get messy. Get crazy. Get excited!

Creativity extends beyond the art store as well. Try new recipes and cook something you haven't before. Follow a recipe verbatim. Make homemade salad dressing, cocktails, bread, and other things you've never tried.

Get creative with your space. Rearrange the furniture, buy new decorations, and try a style you haven't thought of. Start gardening or buy a houseplant. You have been shackled and abused by the narcissist in your life for so long that it might feel strange to do something for yourself, but exploring that side of you can be just the remedy needed to make a full recovery.

80. Changing Lifestyles

If there is ever a time to start a new lifestyle, now is the time! Is there something you have wanted to do for a while? Maybe you want to make a career switch. Perhaps you're interested in going back to school. You might just try veganism or at least eat a nutritious, plant-based diet. Starting something completely new can give you the exact fresh perspective that is needed. Rearranging your bedroom or painting your kitchen can make this fresh start feel more realistic.

Make sure you are doing this for yourself because you want to and not just because you think you should. The point of making lifestyle changes is to replace bad habits with better ones. If you already enjoy your life, you don't necessarily have to change it; now is just a good time to do so if you have already been wishing for a drastic change.

81. Support Systems

Find new sources of support wherever you can. It's straightforward for those recovering from trauma to turn to dangerous or unhealthy vices when seeking to numb that emotional pain. Those who have lived through trauma are more likely to turn to drug or alcohol abuse. They might end up in dangerous situations and experience harmful behavior because of small choices that lead to a negative chain of events.

Maintain support even when you are feeling healthier. Although you might think you've made a full recovery and you're ready to face your most giant demons, you could end up getting triggered. If the support system isn't there, it can be easy to fall back into harmful habits.

Support can start simply online. You can open an anonymous account on a forum site like Reddit to meet like-minded people. You can take it further and look for group therapy. Don't ever be afraid to ask for help and support. You not only need it—you deserve it.

82. Continued Growth

Growth takes time. You don't plant seeds and expect flowers to bloom the next day. You don't give birth and hope the baby to feed itself right away. Growth is also like a roller coaster. Sometimes there are quick bursts and a lot of change happens. Occasionally, you will dip back into old habits. Sometimes the growth is slow and steady.

Never stop nourishing your desire for growth. As humans, we are constantly changing. Even though our minds stop developing after adulthood, that doesn't mean they stop changing forever. There are always transformations, epiphanies, and moments of enlightenment ahead.

You might never hit a point where you can say, "I'm completely healed from my abuse, and the trauma doesn't affect me anymore." It might stay with you forever. But this isn't a bad thing at all! You will eventually realize that your trauma is simply a scar that has helped develop you into the person you are now. You've lived through tough things, and that means you will come out even stronger afterwards.

Always look for ways to let yourself grow, be free, and become the person you are meant to be. If anyone ever tries to stop that from happening, you know exactly how to handle it now.

Conclusion

A Healthy life with a narcissist is impossible. They do not know how to communicate with others in a way that is not manipulative. This is likely because as a child, they could not get their needs met by asking and had to go about it in an underhanded way. Then and as an adult, they continue this behavior. They will likely use stories of childhood tragedies as a way of playing on your sympathy and getting you not to leave them. You can feel compassion for what they endured as a child, but you owe it to yourself not to tolerate abuse from the person they have become as an adult.

This means their time needs to be filled with something else, so they won't have time to think about and contact the person they are trying to distance themselves from. This is the time to make new friends and reconnect with old ones.

A person who is a victim of long-term narcissistic abuse needs some form of psychiatric care because, at this point, they are also mentally unwell. They have likely regressed into a state of learned helplessness and have cultivated a victim mentality. They do not think they can do anything about their situation. They have developed a trauma bond with the narcissist, a term used to describe a victim's psychology repeatedly going back to their abuser. Partially it is because they do not think they deserve better, and they also have the idea of "it's better to live with the evil you do know than face the unknown." This is a thought process they will have to break to escape the cycle of abuse.

Cognitive-behavioral therapy, also known as CBT, is highly effective in treating a person trying to recover from narcissistic abuse. A therapist who practices CBT guides their patients by taking negative thinking patterns that are destructive to one's mental health and transforming them into more positive ones.

The trauma bond is a distorted thinking pattern. The narcissistic abuse victim has become addicted to the positively emotionally charged cycle of their relationship with the narcissist. There are several reasons for this. Constant putdowns have torn down their self-esteem. The narcissist also knows exactly how much abuse their victim can take and when they have to use the love-bombing tactics again.

This creates a feeling that the connection between them is more profound than the ones they had with other people in the past because the two of them have "been through so much." The victim also might have been raised by a narcissist, so they are subconsciously gravitating toward what is familiar.

This is why the narcissist must take up a hobby and do something productive to meet new people. Their past abuser's insults have become a voice in their head, and this voice needs to be eliminated.

For example, if they take up sewing, they will feel a sense of accomplishment when they have created a piece of clothing, which will automatically boost their self-esteem. It will also develop friendships with people who think well of them and show them affection.

Their kind words will eventually challenge the negative ones from their abuser, and ultimately, the thought will cross the person's mind, "should I listen to one person who doesn't like me, or all of these other people who do?"

While this means blocking the victim, you could contact them, but ignore the barrage of calls and messages that will soon follow. You may have the urge to get them again and begin the smear campaign that so many narcissists throw upon their victims when they attempt to leave.

A covert narcissist is exceptionally skilled at starting a smear campaign. They have carefully crafted an image of themselves as helpless victims, and they enjoy assassinating someone else's character. The narcissist will tell others they do not know you as well as they think they do. They will try to convince everyone that you are mentally unstable while masking the mental instability that drives them to do this to yet another person. If you remain unresponsive, everyone will see you as being calm and collected while they are ranting and raving about you. Eventually, no one will want to hear them talk about you anymore.

It is a good idea to connect with people who have shared your experiences. The right group will hold you accountable and talk you out of making mistakes - like breaking the rule of no contact. They will not excuse you. A support group's goal should be to help one another move on, not stay in the same unhappy place.

If you must talk to the person because of children, work, or some other reason, use the tactic known as grey rocking. This technique has its name because the goal is to be as emotionless and uninterested as a grey rock

www.ingramcontent.com/pod-product-compliance
Lightning Source LLC
Chambersburg PA
CBHW071605080526
44588CB00010B/1023